DATA AT SPEED

What Professional Racing Teaches Leaders About Decisions and Performance

MARK RAMSEY, PH.D.

ISBN: 979-8-9953053-0-9 (hardcover)
ISBN: 979-8-9953053-1-6 (paperback)
ISBN: 979-8-9953053-3-0 (B&W paperback)
ISBN: 979-8-9953053-2-3 (digital)

First edition, 2026

Cover photograph by Hector Hernandez Garcia.

Printed in the United States of America.

About the Author

Mark Ramsey, Ph.D. is one of the most experienced data and analytics leaders in the industry. Over more than 35 years, he has advised hundreds of organizations across dozens of industries, helping them use data as a strategic asset to drive significant business value. Over the past decade, he has advised five of the top ten pharmaceutical companies in using data and analytics to drive transformational changes in drug Research and Development.

As Managing Partner of Ramsey International, Mark and his team help global organizations design and deliver modern data ecosystems, with a keen focus on the use of generative AI. He is a sought-after keynote speaker at major corporate and industry events, known for translating the complexities of data strategy into practical, actionable insight. His career includes pioneering roles as the first R&D Chief Data & Analytics Officer at GlaxoSmithKline, the first Chief Data Officer at Samsung Telecommunications America, and the leader of IBM's global Business Analytics & Optimization practice.

A master inventor, Dr. Ramsey holds 30 patents in data and analytics, an MBA, and a Ph.D. in Applied Computer Science.

Dedication

For Trina.

I selected 92 as my car number for the year we got married, but the truth is that every lap I have ever turned was made possible by you. You never asked for a life that included being in the grandstands watching for your husband's car, not knowing whether the silence meant he was on the back straight or in the wall. You lived every race, every risk, every moment of uncertainty, and you came back to the next one.

You found your own way to manage the stress. You discovered meditation, and it became a passion that has shaped your life as profoundly as racing has shaped mine. What you may not know is that racing is my meditation. When I am in the car at speed, there is no room for anything else. No emails, no strategy decks, no quarterly reviews. The car demands total concentration, absolute presence, and in that demand, it gives me the same thing your practice gives you: a clear mind.

Thank you for your unwavering support, even when the why was hard to understand. This book, and everything it represents, would not exist without you.

CONTENTS

Foreword

It is a privilege to contribute this foreword. Over the past two decades of hosting the Annual CDOIQ Symposium, previously held at MIT, I have had the honor of witnessing hundreds of presentations delivered by some of the world's most accomplished data leaders. Many have been excellent. A few have been truly memorable.

Mark Ramsey's presentation at the Symposium was one such rare moment. The audience set aside distractions and engaged with full attention as he drew a striking parallel between professional motorsports and the leadership of data-driven organizations. His synthesis offered a novel framework that emphasized precision, resilience, and strategic adaptation—qualities that resonate deeply with the Symposium's mission to advance the practice of data leadership.

What makes both the presentation and this book so compelling is the extraordinary depth of expertise Mark brings. With more than thirty-five years at the forefront of data, analytics, and artificial intelligence—including pioneering leadership roles at Samsung, GSK, and IBM—he has architected and scaled global data organizations, secured thirty patents, and cultivated a rare, firsthand understanding of how the pressures of real-time, high-stakes decision-making mirror the challenges every enterprise faces in its pursuit of genuine data-driven transformation.

Across decades of research and writing, I have observed the Chief Data Officer role undergo a profound evolution—from its origins as a technical function focused on governance and compliance to its current stature as a strategic leadership position at the center of organizational change. Today's

CDO is expected not merely to steward data assets, but to drive revenue growth, enable artificial intelligence, and shape competitive strategy. This transformation underscores the necessity of a book such as Data at Speed*: the frameworks required by CDOs are no longer confined to technical domains but extend to the demands of leadership under pressure and the orchestration of enterprise-wide transformation.*

Data at Speed *presents a rigorously constructed framework for understanding the organizational imperatives of data-driven leadership. Drawing on the metaphor of the racing team—an enterprise that is high-performing, relentlessly data-intensive, and intolerant of error—Mark illuminates the principles that distinguish organizations that merely espouse the value of data from those that truly compete with it. Within this model, he addresses the evolving role of the Chief Data Officer, the critical importance of real-time analytics, the enduring challenge of cultivating trust in data, the necessity of cross-functional collaboration, and the leadership courage required to make consequential decisions when information is imperfect and time is scarce.*

It is with the utmost confidence that I commend this book to you without reservation.

Richard Y. Wang, Ph.D.
Former professor, Massachusetts Institute of Technology
Professor Emeritus, University of Arkansas, Little Rock
Former Deputy CDO & Chief DQ Officer, Pentagon
Former CDO, State of Arkansas
Founder & Executive Director of Chief Data Officer & Information Quality (CDOIQ) ProgramFounder Certified CDO (CCDO) Program
Founder CDOIQ Society

Part I

Life in the Fast Lane:

Data and Analytics in Professional Motorsports

CHAPTER 1

The Green Flag

I walked into the MIT Chief Data Officer and Information Quality Symposium wearing a racing suit.

Presenting at the MIT CDOIQ Symposium in my racing suit.

Not a business suit. Not a blue sport coat. A full, fire-retardant Nomex racing suit, the kind you wear when you strap yourself into a car traveling at over a hundred miles per hour and hope that everything you've prepared, everything your team has built, and everything the data is telling you will be enough to keep you competitive. And alive.

The first time I had raced in that suit was at Daytona International Speedway for the IMSA 4-hour endurance race during the weekend of the

IMSA Rolex 24-hour race. It was overwhelming to be on a track of this magnitude for the first time amongst forty-two other cars, with rubber flying from the tires, and cars having incidents around me. We survived the challenge and finished in the middle of the field.

The audience, a room full of chief data officers and analytics leaders from some of the most sophisticated organizations in the world, did not quite know what to make of it. I could see the looks. Some were amused. Some were confused. A few clearly thought I had lost my mind. I had their attention, and that was the point. Because what I was about to tell them was something I had spent years learning in two very different arenas, and I needed them to understand that the connection between those arenas was not a metaphor. It was not an analogy stretched to the breaking point for the sake of a keynote presentation. It was real. The lessons were real. And the failures, the spectacular, expensive, humbling failures, were very, very real.

After decades in the business world, I built a professional racing team called Big Data in Action. I will say that again, because it sounds like something a marketing department would dream up after too many energy drinks. I created and funded a professional motorsport racing program to demonstrate what a best-in-class data and analytics ecosystem could do when the stakes were immediate, the feedback loops were tight, and the margin between victory and disaster was measured in tenths of a second.

We raced in the IMSA Michelin Pilot Challenge series in 2018 and 2019, as well as the SRO GT4 Americas and TransAm series in 2019. IMSA is the premier sanctioning body for sports car racing in North America, and the Michelin Pilot Challenge is its production-based class, one step below the top-tier WeatherTech SportsCar Championship. SRO GT4 Americas is an international series for the same class of production-based race cars. TransAm is one of the oldest road racing series in the United States, dating back to 1966. We were competing in endurance events – two-hour races, four-hour races – with multiple drivers sharing a single car, making real-time decisions based on data streaming from dozens of sensors while simultaneously managing tire degradation, fuel strategy, and the unpredictable behavior of forty other cars on a track designed to punish mistakes.

We campaigned a Mercedes-AMG GT4 as Car 92 during those seasons, the year my wife and I were married, and I wanted to make a nod to her in this program.

Car 92, the Big Data in Action Mercedes-AMG GT4, at Daytona International Speedway. The livery put the program's data mission on the track for every race.

With co-driver and coach Alexandre Prémat and the Big Data in Action Mercedes-AMG GT4.

Today I race Car 592 in the Spring Mountain Sportscar Series, a regional series based at Spring Mountain Motor Resort in Pahrump, Nevada, the longest road course in the United States and the second longest in the world behind only the Nürburgring. Most months you will find me on the Charleston Peak circuit. I also compete in the NASA (National Auto Sport Association, not the space agency) 6-hour endurance race at Utah Motorsports Campus. Since 92 was already taken in the Spring Mountain series, 592 was the natural choice since we were married in May. The car is a KTM X-BOW GT2, a 600-horsepower carbon fiber monocoque machine that does zero to sixty in three seconds.

Car 592, the KTM X-BOW GT2, on track at Spring Mountain Motor Resort. (Photo courtesy of Spring Mountain Motor Resort and Country Club.)

The KTM has its own family connection. My father-in-law, John, was an early employee of KTM in Austria in the 1950s, and I have the Austrian flag on the car as a nod to that history. I will tell you more about that connection, and the remarkable ride it led to decades later, in Chapter 11.

This book is about what I learned at the intersection of racing and business. More exactly, it is about what professional motorsports can teach any organization about building and extracting value from data and analytics programs. What surprised me most is that **the challenges are identical**. The patterns of failure are the same. The organizational dynamics that derail a racing team's data program are the same dynamics that derail a pharmaceutical or telecommunication company's data program too. I know this because I have led data programs in all those industries. I spent over thirty-five years doing it, from IBM to Samsung to GSK, building data organizations at scale across dozens of industries. You have read the bio. What it does not tell you is why any of that matters for this book.

None of it prepared me for what the racetrack would teach me about data.

Why Racing?

The question I get most often is the obvious one: Why? Why would a data executive with a perfectly respectable career in corporate analytics decide to go racing? And why would he frame it as a data program rather than what it plainly appears to be: a midlife crisis with better sponsorship?

The answer starts with a problem I had been wrestling with for years. Building a big data and analytics solution is difficult. Anyone who has done it knows this. It takes a long time. It requires the coordination of dozens of technologies and the alignment of organizational stakeholders who often have competing priorities. It demands specialized talent and the patience to iterate through failures that can feel endless. I had built these solutions at some of the largest companies in the world, and even with vast resources and executive sponsorship, the path from vision to value was never straight and never easy.

Building a data and analytics solution that delivers in motorsports is something else entirely. It is a significant challenge on a different order of magnitude, not because the data volumes are larger (though in Formula 1 they certainly are), but because the consequences of getting it wrong are immediate and visceral.

In a corporate setting, a flawed analytics model might lead to a suboptimal marketing campaign or a missed quarterly target. The damage is real but diffuse. It shows up in next quarter's earnings call. There is time to course-correct, to commission another study, to schedule a meeting about the meeting.

On a racetrack, a flawed analytics model can put a car into a wall at over a hundred miles per hour. There is no quarterly review. There is no second opinion. The data was either right, or the car was on a flatbed.

That contrast is the reason this book exists. Racing compresses the entire data-to-decision cycle into a timeframe that exposes every weakness in your approach. The feedback loop is not measured in quarters or fiscal years. It is measured in laps. Sometimes in corners.

Boardroom Translation

In a corporation, a data failure shows up in next quarter's earnings call. On a racetrack, it shows up in the tire barrier at 130 mph. The difference is not severity — it is speed of feedback. The organizations that build faster feedback loops between data and decisions gain the same advantage the racetrack gives a driver: you learn what works before it is too late to change course.

That immediacy is what makes motorsports the perfect laboratory for data and analytics. Every assumption is tested in real time. Every model is validated against physics. Every decision has a measurable outcome within minutes, not months. The emotional stakes, the visceral experience of sitting in a car and feeling the consequences of your data strategy, create a kind of learning that no conference room will ever replicate.

There was another reason, too, one that was less analytical and more personal. I love racing. I have always loved racing.

Growing up in central Ohio, I lived near National Trails Raceway, where each year the NHRA Spring Nationals were held. That drag strip was my introduction to motorsports. I watched the greats of the sport in the 1970s and 1980s: Shirley Muldowney, Connie Kalitta, John Force, Don "Big Daddy" Garlits, Don Prudhomme, Kenny Bernstein. Top fuel and funny car drivers who were larger than life. I did not just watch, though. National Trails had amateur weekends, "run what you bring," and that is where I learned to drive. I had a 1968 Dodge Coronet R/T with a 440 Magnum engine and a four-speed manual transmission. I not only learned to drag race in that car, I learned how to rebuild the engine and transmission, because when you are learning to race, you are also learning how to break things. My dad and I spent countless hours working together to have that car set up to race. I was able to run a 13.08-second quarter mile in that Coronet, which was amazing given the weight of the car with that powertrain.

I always dreamed of road racing, but the closest road course was several hours away, and I never had the chance. Then in 2012, I attended the Bob Bondurant Racing School in Phoenix, and that started me on the path.

Learning the racing line in a Bondurant Corvette and Formula Mazda. The school's multi-day programs take you from fundamentals through high-performance driving.

In 2016, I began wheel-to-wheel racing in the Exotics Racing series at Las Vegas Motor Speedway with French Mitjet race cars. Exotics Racing still offers supercar and racecar driving experiences, though they no longer run the racing series where I got my start.

My Exotics Racing Mitjet at Las Vegas Motor Speedway, 2017. Car 68 with the Ramsey International livery. This is where I learned wheel-to-wheel racing.

Racing the Mitjet at WeatherTech Raceway Laguna Seca.

From there, the progression to professional endurance racing with the Big Data in Action program was a natural, if ambitious, next step.

With Trina in the Big Data in Action paddock at Laguna Seca.

And when you find something that combines your deepest professional expertise with your deepest personal passion, you do not walk away from it. You figure out how to make it work.

The Cultural Moment

The timing was not accidental. When I launched the Big Data in Action racing program, motorsports was undergoing a transformation that mirrored the transformation happening in enterprise data. Formula 1, the pinnacle of the sport, had become a cultural phenomenon, particularly in the United States, and the catalyst was, appropriately enough, data presented as storytelling.

Netflix's *Drive to Survive* series, which debuted in 2019, did something remarkable. It took a sport that most Americans viewed as an incomprehensible European pastime and turned it into must-watch television. The transformation has been massive: there are now three United States Grand Prix races on the calendar, and millions of American fans have embraced what was historically a European sport. The show understood that racing is not really about cars going fast. Racing is about people making decisions under pressure, managing risks, navigating organizational politics (every F1 team is, at its core, a high-stakes technology organization), and dealing with the emotional consequences when those decisions go right or catastrophically wrong.

That is an exact description of what it feels like to lead a data program in any large organization.

Drive to Survive only hinted at the data story underneath. The real story, the one that the Netflix cameras rarely showed, was far more interesting. In Chapter 3, I will take you inside Formula 1's data operation in detail – the scale is staggering, and the principles are identical to what we were doing with Big Data in Action, just with several more zeros on the budget. The fundamental question at the center of both programs was the same: How do you build a data ecosystem that turns raw information into competitive advantage?

The Ecosystem

Like every serious data program I have built, Big Data in Action required multiple technologies working together — each contributing a specific capability, all integrated into a coherent whole. Cloudera CDP formed the foundation, underpinning the entire platform. Modak brought their Nabu product, which builds dynamic Spark pipelines to load and consolidate data quickly; I had relied on Nabu across large-scale enterprise implementations in other industries, and it handled the racing environment's mix of real-time telemetry streams alongside batch data from video analysis, weather stations, and historical performance databases. Tamr handled AI-driven data resolution, reconciling the inevitable conflicts that arise whenever you bring disparate sources into a common model. Because even on a racetrack, data quality matters enormously. Bad data does not just lead to bad decisions; it leads to bad decisions at over a hundred miles per hour.

Universal challenges showed up here too: integrating technologies that were not designed for each other, keeping pipelines reliable under pressure, and making sure the analytical outputs reached the people who needed to act on them. The physics are different. The organizational dynamics are not.

The Thrill and the Agony

There is a photograph I keep on my desk. It shows me standing on a podium after a race, holding a trophy, grinning like a child who has just been told that summer vacation will never end. The car behind me is still hot, the tires are shredded, and there's champagne dripping off my racing suit.

On the podium at Daytona International Speedway in the TransAm series. The photograph I keep on my desk.

There is another photograph I keep nearby. It shows my car crumpled, the front end demolished, grass caked on the front splitter from spinning into the infield. Months of preparation and significant financial investment converted into scrap metal in two seconds.

Car 92 after the Road America crash in the IMSA Series. The other photograph I keep nearby.

The thrill of victory. The agony of defeat. In motorsports, these are not clichés. They are on Friday and Saturday of the same week.

And here is what I need you to understand: this is no different than data programs. Every data leader who has ever built a pipeline that failed at three in the morning on the night before a board presentation knows the feeling. Racing makes the moments more vivid and more consequential. The emotional arc is identical, and the lessons for navigating it are directly transferable.

What This Book Will Cover

The racing we did was endurance racing: events lasting two hours, four hours, sometimes longer. Unlike a sprint race where a single driver pushes as hard as possible for a short duration, endurance racing requires managing resources over time. Multiple drivers share the car. Tire management becomes as important as raw speed. Fuel strategy can win or lose a race. Weather changes can invalidate an entire race plan in minutes. The car that crosses the finish line first is not always the car that was fastest. It is the car that was most consistently fast while avoiding catastrophic failure.

That is also an exact description of managing a multi-year data transformation program. Most organizations do not fail because they lack talented people, sophisticated technology, or ambitious goals. They fail because they underestimate the complexity of sustaining performance over time. They focus on individual initiatives rather than the system as a whole. They optimize for short-term wins while neglecting the resources, dependencies, and external factors that ultimately determine long-term success. Like an endurance race, a transformation program is won through a series of thousands of small decisions, each informed by data, each contributing incrementally to the final outcome.

The parallels between endurance racing and enterprise data strategy are far deeper than they first appear. Both require turning overwhelming complexity into manageable decisions. Both depend on understanding not only what is happening now, but what is likely to happen next. And both reward finding information others overlook and acting on it faster. The principles in this book emerged from those shared realities.

The Five Racing Principles

Over the course of this book, I will introduce five principles drawn directly from how professional racing teams use data to win. These are not abstract theories. They are practices I have used in racing and applied in boardrooms across industries, and they form the core framework of this book.

Principle 1: Decompose Your Key Metrics. A driver does not think about "going fast through the corner." A driver breaks the corner into six sub-actions: braking point, trail braking, turn-in, apex, exit, and acceleration. Your organization's key metrics deserve the same treatment. Revenue, churn, time-to-market: these are corners, not numbers. Break them apart and you will find where the time is hiding.

Principle 2: Predict and Monitor Your Resources. Endurance racing teams do not just track their lap times. They monitor fuel, tires, car health, and driver fatigue, because running out of any one of them ends the race. Most organizations predict business outcomes but neglect to predict the resources required to deliver them.

Principle 3: Expand Your Use of External Data. Every top racing team builds its own weather models rather than relying on the same forecast everyone else receives. In business, the organizations that win are the ones that look beyond their own walls for data that creates a genuine competitive advantage.

Principle 4: Find Unique Data Sources. The data you need may already exist in an industry that has no idea it is valuable to you. The best racing teams, and the best data organizations, are relentless about finding information that nobody else has thought to look for.

Principle 5: Mine Your History Creatively. Racing teams load years of historical data to predict competitor strategies and build driver profiles. The most valuable insights in historical data are often hidden in the gaps, the white space between events, not in the events themselves. **White Space Analysis**, a framework for finding competitive advantage in the gaps that nobody measures, may be the single most transferable idea in this book.

In Part II, each principle is explained in its own chapter, with practical frameworks you can apply starting the week you finish reading.

This book is not a technical manual. It is also not a racing memoir, though I will share stories from the track when they illuminate a larger point. What it is, I hope, is a bridge – a way of seeing the challenges of enterprise data and analytics through a lens that makes them more intuitive and more solvable.

Who This Book Is For

I wrote this book for three audiences, and I think the overlap between them is larger than most people realize.

The first audience is **data and analytics leaders**: Chief Data Officers, Chief Analytics Officers, and the teams building data programs inside organizations. If that is you, this book will give you a new framework for thinking about the challenges you face every day. The racing model is not just a metaphor. It is a working example of everything you are trying to build: real-time decision-making, trust in data, cross-functional collaboration under pressure, and resilience when things go wrong.

The second audience is **business executives** who depend on data programs but do not lead them. If you have ever wondered why your data investments have not delivered the returns you expected, or why your analytics team speaks a different language than the rest of the organization, this book will help. The racing parallels make the concepts concrete in a way that traditional business writing often does not.

The third audience is **racing enthusiasts and drivers** at any level. Whether you are a club racer running weekend track days, someone who has always been curious about what separates good drivers from great ones, or a motorsport fan who wants to understand the data layer beneath the sport you love, there is a lot here for you. The chapters on trail braking, tire management, race strategy, and telemetry analysis are not just analogies for business concepts. They are real racing instruction, grounded in data, and I have tried to explain them at a level that is both accessible and technically honest. If you are a racer, the data techniques in this book can make you faster. If you are a fan, they will change how you watch a race.

What connects all three audiences is a simple idea: the best decisions, whether at over a hundred miles per hour or in a boardroom, come from people who know how to use data without being paralyzed by it. That is what racing teaches, and that is what this book is about.

The green flag is waving. Let's go.

PIT BOARD **CHAPTER 1**

FEEDBACK LOOPS
LAPS
NOT QUARTERS

Key Lesson: Racing compresses the entire data-to-decision cycle into a timeframe that exposes every weakness in your approach. The feedback loop is measured in laps, not quarters.

Business Translation: The patterns that derail a racing team's data program are the same patterns that derail any organization's data program. The physics are different; organizational dynamics are not.

Racer Tip: If you are considering building a data-driven racing program at any level, start with the five principles outlined in this chapter - they scale from club racing to professional endurance.

Monday Action: Identify the single metric in your organization where the feedback loops between data and decision is longest. That is your biggest opportunity to compress.

CHAPTER 2

The Data-Driven Cockpit

The first time I truly understood the power of data in racing, I was sitting in a trailer behind the pit lane at a regional circuit, staring at a laptop screen, watching two versions of myself drive the same car around the same track.

Here is what that means. There is a piece of software called MoTeC i2, the industry-standard motorsports data analysis platform used by professional teams worldwide, that allows you to compare laps side by side. MoTeC i2 features customizable plots, graphs, and histograms, 2D and 3D graphing, scatter plots, and synchronized multi-camera video overlay with logged telemetry data. It can analyze throttle, brake, and steering input alongside tire data, fuel consumption, g-forces, and suspension data with impressive precision. On the screen, you see two video windows, each showing an onboard camera view. One window shows your car on one lap. The other window shows your car on a different lap. The videos are synchronized to the track position, not to time, so you can see exactly where you are on the circuit at each moment and compare what you did differently.

In the case that opened my eyes, I was not comparing two of my own laps. I was comparing my best lap to a lap driven by my professional racing coach, Alexandre Prémat, around the same circuit in the same car on the same day. Alex is a French professional driver with factory-level experience in DTM, Le Mans, and GP2. He coached me from 2016 to 2020, and his ability to extract performance from a car was the benchmark I measured myself against. My current coach, since 2022, is Cole Loftsgard, an American sports car driver who worked his way up from grassroots competition into a fulltime professional.

The numbers at the top of the screen told a story that was both humbling and illuminating. His lap was 1.24 seconds faster than mine.

If you do not come from a motorsports background, 1.24 seconds might not sound like much. It is the amount of time it takes to blink twice. In everyday life, it is nothing. On a racetrack, it is an eternity. In competitive racing, a difference of 1.24 seconds between two cars is the difference between standing on the podium and finishing in the middle of the pack. It is, as we say in the sport, like finishing yesterday.

The raw time difference was not the interesting part, though. The interesting part was *where* the time was gained and lost, and what the data revealed about why.

Two Kinds of Speed

The MoTeC i2 display showed more than just video. Below the video windows, a speed trace charted both laps - let us call them the blue lap (mine) and the red lap (my coach) - as continuous lines on a graph. The horizontal axis represented distance around the track. The vertical axis represented speed. Every straight, every braking zone, every corner, every acceleration point was visible as a pattern in the data.

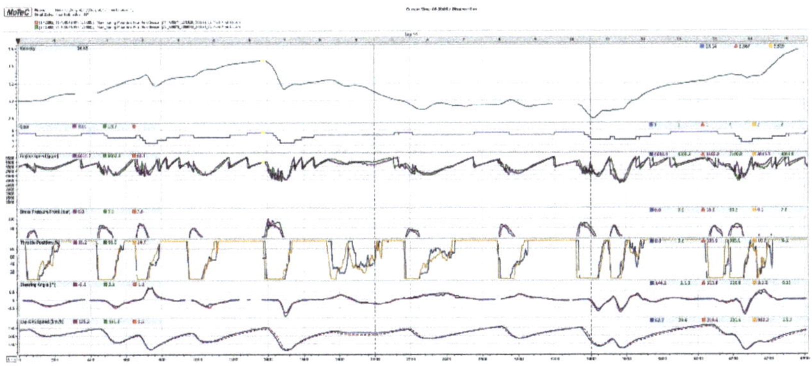

Figure 2.1: A MoTeC i2 lap comparison. Two laps are overlaid — the speed, throttle, brake, gear, engine speed, and steering traces of each run are charted together along the length of the lap, so where one driver gains or loses time becomes visible immediately.

The speed trace is a beautiful piece of analytical visualization, and I say that as someone who has spent decades looking at dashboards and reports. It compresses an enormous amount of information into an immediately readable format. Speed climbing on the straights as the car accelerates toward its maximum velocity. Speed dropping sharply at the braking zones where the driver stamps on the brake pedal before entering a corner. The minimum speed at the apex of each turn, the slowest point in each corner, which is paradoxically one of the most important numbers in all of racing. Speed building again as the driver exits the corner and gets back on the throttle.

When I looked at the blue line and the red line together, something unexpected jumped out. Through most of the lap, through the first two-thirds of the circuit, my blue line was above the red line. I was carrying more speed through corners. I was braking later. I was faster. Not by a lot, but measurably, consistently faster. If the lap had ended at the two-thirds mark, I would have been almost three seconds ahead.

Three seconds ahead. Same car, same tires, same conditions. For someone who was comparing himself to a professional, this was thrilling. It suggested that all those hours of practice, all that study of racing lines and braking techniques, had been paying off.

And then I looked at the last third of the lap.

Where the Time Goes

The circuit we were running had a characteristic shared by many racetracks: the final corner led directly onto the longest straight. This is a common design philosophy in circuit layout. The main straight, where cars reach their highest speeds and where most overtaking happens, begins at the exit of the last turn. This means that the last corner of the lap is, from a data perspective, the most consequential corner on the circuit. Your exit speed from that corner determines your speed for the entire length of the straight. A difference of just two or three miles per hour at the corner exit translates to a much larger difference by the time you reach the braking zone at the end of the straight.

My data showed exactly what had happened. Approaching the final corner, I braked too early. Not by much. Twenty meters, the length of a few cars. Those twenty meters meant I arrived at the apex of the corner at a lower speed. A lower apex speed meant I had to wait longer before I could get back on the throttle. Waiting longer on the throttle meant I carried less speed onto the straight. Less speed onto the longest straight on the circuit meant that the three seconds I had built up over the previous two-thirds of the lap evaporated. Not slowly. Completely. In one corner, I gave back everything I had earned, and then some, finishing 1.24 seconds behind.

Alex, looking at the same data, summarized the lesson with the kind of economy that comes from years of experience. "Position of the car means when you can start going back to the gas," he said. "Gas is your friend. The brake, you use when you must."

That sentence contains more wisdom about data-driven decision-making than most business books I have read. To understand why, you need to understand what was happening in that final corner – and that requires a deeper look at the physics of how a race car turns.

Why Brakes Don't Do What You Think They Do

Here is the first thing you need to unlearn: the brake pedal is not primarily there to slow the car down.

Yes, brakes decelerate a vehicle. In racing, though, the brake pedal serves a far more important purpose. When you press the brake, you transfer the weight of the car forward, onto the front tires. This weight transfer (the shift of the car's mass toward the front axle under deceleration) is what allows the front tires to grip the road surface and rotate the car into the turn. Without that weight on the front, the car simply will not turn. Press the brake, and the nose dives. The front tires compress into the asphalt. The contact patch (the few square inches of rubber touching the road) is loaded with additional force. The car becomes steerable.

Release the brake too quickly, and the weight shifts rearward. The front tires unload. The car goes from responsive to numb in a fraction of a second. The act of braking and the act of turning must overlap because the weight transfer is what makes turning possible.

A tire has a finite grip budget – you can spend that budget on braking or on cornering, but not both at full demand simultaneously. Exceed the budget and the car ignores your steering input entirely, pushing straight ahead in what drivers call understeer (where the front tires lose traction and the car plows wide of the intended line). On a racetrack, every corner is a negotiation with physics, and the tires are the currency.

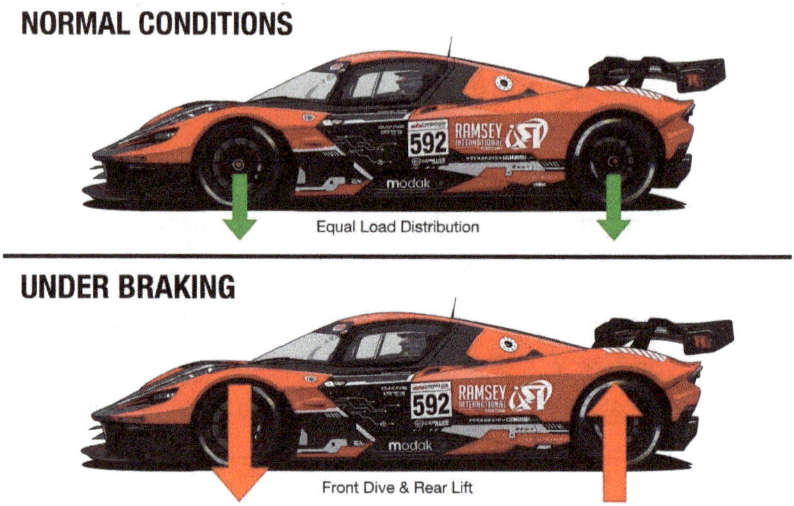

Figure 2.2: Weight Transfer and Brake Physics, showing how braking transfers weight to the front tires, creating the grip that makes turning possible, and how the grip budget is split between braking and cornering forces.

The Late Apex: Doing the Opposite of What Feels Right

If I asked a room full of intelligent people how to drive the fastest line through a 90-degree corner, most would sketch a wide, symmetrical arc clipping the geometric center. When I give this presentation to rooms full of Chief Data Officers, they universally converge on that answer. It is also the slowest way to drive that corner, by multiple tenths of a second.

The fast way through is counterintuitive. First, you approach in a straight line and brake hard, later than feels safe, because braking in a straight line is where the tire gives you maximum deceleration. Then comes the critical transition: you are still on the brakes, and you begin to turn. You start with 99 percent brake pressure, then slowly release the pedal as you increase steering angle, feeding the grip budget from "mostly braking" to "mostly turning" in a smooth, continuous transfer. Racing instructors call this trail braking (the technique of gradually releasing brake pressure while simultaneously increasing steering input), and it is the single most important technique in road racing.

Because you braked late and trail-braked into the turn, you have pushed the apex (the closest point to the inside of the corner) much later than the geometric midpoint – to the two-thirds point or even later. This is what racing drivers call a late apex. The car is not tracing a smooth curve. It is doing something more like a hockey stick: a late, hard entry followed by a sharp rotation and then an early, aggressive exit.

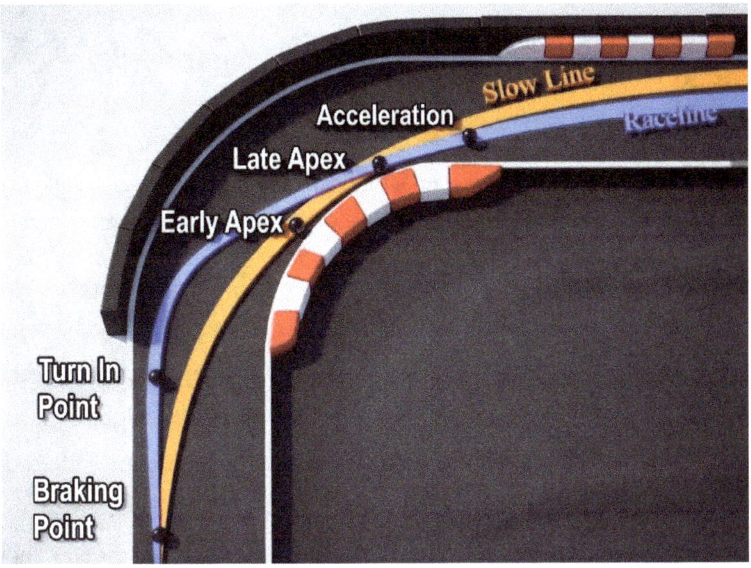

Figure 2.3: The Intuitive Line vs. The Racing Line, illustrating the difference between the symmetrical arc most people envision and the late-apex, trail-braking technique that produces faster lap times.

*Car 592 at the apex of a corner at Spring Mountain. The late-apex technique in practice — the car is already **pointed** toward the exit, ready for early throttle application. (Photo courtesy of Spring Mountain Motor Resort and Country Club.)*

The payoff: because the apex is late, the car is already pointed down the next straightaway sooner. The driver can get back on the throttle earlier, which means higher speed down the entire following straight. The time gained is not in the corner itself. It is in the straight that comes after. This is the insight that changes everything: the fastest way through a corner is not to go through the corner faster. It is to get back on the gas sooner coming out.

There is a moment in every well-executed corner when the driver's feet are performing a kind of ballet. The left foot modulates the brake with the precision of a concert pianist while the right foot is already beginning to apply throttle. For a brief instant, the car is simultaneously decelerating and accelerating, the weight balanced perfectly, the tire grip being transferred from braking through cornering into acceleration in one seamless motion. It is one of the most demanding cognitive and physical tasks a human being can perform, and data makes it possible – not in the moment, but through the countless hours of telemetry review that rewire the driver's neural pathways until the three-meter braking point adjustment feels like instinct.

This is the ultimate expression of data-driven performance: not data replacing human judgment, but data making human judgment better.

What the Data Revealed

Now going back to my speed trace comparison with Alex. The data told exactly this story. I was carrying more speed through the middle of corners – the intuitive approach – but compromising my exits. Alex's late-apex technique, the counterintuitive approach that feels slower through the middle, set him up for earlier throttle application and higher speed down every straight. Speed through the corner is not the same as fast through the corner.

Structured Meets Unstructured

What MoTeC i2 was doing in that trailer was integrating structured and unstructured data for comparative analysis. The structured data – speed traces, braking data, throttle position, GPS coordinates, sector times (the lap broken into timed segments between fixed points on the circuit) – was numerical and precise, captured by sensors at high frequency. The unstructured data was the video: two camera feeds showing where the car was positioned relative to the curbing, how the car's body language changed under different inputs.

Neither type told the full story alone. The speed trace showed that I was slower in the final corner, but it could not show why in a way that was actionable. The video showed the visual experience but could not quantify the difference. Together, synchronized by track position, they told a complete, actionable story. I could see the speed trace dropping earlier and simultaneously watch my foot moving to the brake at a point where my coach's foot was still flat on the throttle.

If you are a club racer, this technique is something you can start doing today. MoTeC's i2 software is free to download, and most modern data loggers export in a format it can read.

This is the model every organization should aspire to: integrating different types of data to create insights that neither type could produce alone. At GlaxoSmithKline, some of the most powerful analytical moments came when we combined structured clinical trial data with unstructured physician notes. The pattern is the same. The magic is in the integration.

Batch and Real-Time: Two Modes of Insight

The analysis I have just described was performed in batch mode – after the fact. I drove, came back to the pits, and sat down to review the data. In a practice session, this is fine. Batch analysis is how you learn. The cycle time (drive, review, adjust, drive) is the fundamental learning loop of motorsports, mapping directly to the build-measure-learn loop in modern software development.

The IMSA series does not allow active telemetry during races, limiting our data capture to roughly twenty percent of what an F1 team generates. That constraint forced creative approaches and frankly made us better analysts. For those running club races under similar restrictions, take heart: the batch review process is where the biggest gains live

During a race where telemetry is allowed, something very different happens. The data streams in real time. Picture a four-hour endurance race. The race engineer monitors live visualizations of every car's position, tracking lap times, calculating gaps, projecting pit stop windows (the range of laps during which pitting is strategically optimal). Decisions are being made in seconds. Getting it wrong means losing the race.

The Two Modes in Your Organization

Every organization needs both modes. Batch analysis is how you understand what happened and why. Real-time analytics is how you respond to what is happening now. Most organizations I have worked with are far stronger at batch – looking backward. Real-time analytics, the ability to act on current conditions, is where most struggle. Not because the technology is unavailable, but because of trust.

In racing, the driver trusts the engineer to deliver a clear instruction: "Pit this lap." "Push now." "Save fuel, we're going long." The relationship between data and action has been compressed to its essential minimum. How many organizations operate this way? Very few. Most have built the infrastructure for real-time data but schedule a meeting to discuss what the dashboard is showing. No race engineer would tolerate that cadence.

The Data Nobody Sees

Racing fans see the overtakes, the pit stops, the celebrations and crashes. They do not see the telemetry streams, the speed traces, the tire degradation models. Most organizations have the same challenge. The work of data teams is often invisible: the pipelines that run reliably, the data quality processes that catch errors. This invisibility leads to undervaluation. If the organization cannot see the work, it will not fund the work. Every organization should strive to make its data work as visible and as clearly connected to outcomes as it is in a racing team.

Inside the War Room

There is a room you never see during a race broadcast. It is not glamorous. There are no roaring engines, no checkered flags. It is a folding table behind the pit wall, or a cramped enclosure filled with monitors, cables, and the quiet intensity of people making decisions that will determine whether the last four months of preparation amount to a victory or a retirement. This is the war room.

The Marching Ants

During a race, the sanctioning body makes certain data available to every team. One of the most important displays is deceptively simple: a graphic of the track layout with small circles representing every car in the field, all moving around the circuit in real time. Engineers call them "marching ants" because, from a distance, that is exactly what they look like. A procession of tiny dots tracing the outline of the circuit, each one representing a multi-hundred-thousand-dollar machine being piloted at the limit by a human being strapped into a carbon fiber tub.

Our car, Car 92, was highlighted on this display, and I could see at a glance where we sat relative to every other car on the track. Who was ahead, who was behind. Whether the car in front was pulling away or whether we were closing the gap. The display updated continuously, and while it might seem like a basic visualization, the information density was impressive. In a field of forty or fifty cars spread around a multi-mile circuit, you could immediately assess the competitive landscape.

The marching ants were just the beginning. Layered on top of that positional data was a continuous stream of performance information. The race organization provided lap times for every car in the field, updated each time a car crossed the start-finish line. You could see who was fast, who was struggling, who had just posted a personal best, and who had suddenly slowed, perhaps indicating a mechanical problem or a driver error.

The system also tracked pit stops: when each car came in, how long it spent in the pits, and what could be inferred about what work was done. A thirty-second stop likely meant fuel only. A sixty-second stop probably included tires. Anything longer suggested a mechanical issue. This information was gold, because it revealed your competitors' strategies in real time.

Our engineer, sitting behind the pit wall with multiple screens and a headset connecting directly to me in the car, was synthesizing all this simultaneously. He had a mind that could process data the way a jazz musician processes chord changes. Comparative lap times. Gap analysis. Fuel consumption calculations. Tire degradation models. And above all, the strategic implications of every piece of information. You do not need a full-time race engineer to get this kind of value. At club endurance events, a spotter or crew chief with a laptop running the timing feed and a radio can provide the same strategic layer. Someone watching the gaps, tracking when competitors pit, and thinking about fuel windows will make you faster even if the setup is just a folding chair and a Wi-Fi connection.

He would key the radio and say something like, "Car 22 has pitted, you're now P3, gap to P2 is 4.2 seconds and closing, fuel is good for twelve more laps, keep your pace." In that one transmission was the distillation of dozens of data streams into a single actionable message. I did not need to know the raw data. I needed to know what to do. The engineer's job was to be the analytical layer between the data and the decision, to take the flood of information and reduce it to clarity.

This was not a dashboard someone checked once an hour. This was a continuous, flowing river of data being interpreted in real time, with decisions that had to be made in minutes or sometimes seconds. All this comparative data flooding in, all feeding into decisions that could not wait. Analytics at its most immediate and consequential.

Car 92 pushing through a corner at Watkins Glen in the SRO GT4 Series. Every position, every gap, every closing rate feeds back to the war room in real time.

The Four Resources

In endurance racing, whether it is a two-hour sprint or the legendary 24 Hours of Le Mans, every strategic decision comes down to the management of four critical resources: fuel, tires, car health, and the driver.

Each of these resources deplete over time, each at a different rate depending on conditions, and each has a failure mode that ranges from inconvenient to catastrophic. The engineer's job, and by extension, the entire analytics apparatus supporting the team, is to monitor and optimize the consumption of these four resources in the context of a competitive environment where everyone else is doing the same calculation.

Fuel is the easiest resource to model mathematically. A car burns fuel at a rate that is predictable based on engine speed, throttle application, and ambient conditions. Teams know how much fuel is in the car at the start of the race and have a good estimate of the burn rate. That makes it possible to predict with reasonable precision when the fuel supply will run out. The strategic question is not whether a refueling stop will be required, but when it should occur and how much fuel should be added.

Running out of fuel on a racetrack is not a pleasant experience. I can tell you this from firsthand experience. The engine does not give you a polite low-fuel warning like your daily driver. It simply stops. Momentum carries you forward for a few seconds, and then you are rolling to a halt on a live racetrack while cars scream past you at race speed, and you are trying to coast to a safe location while your engineer is on the radio calmly explaining that this was not part of the plan. Fuel management is a problem you solve with data and discipline, not with optimism.

Tires are a more complex variable. Unlike fuel, which is depleted in a linear fashion, tire degradation is nonlinear and depends on a vast number of factors: track temperature, driving style, car setup, the specific compound of rubber, even whether you are running in clean air or in the turbulent air behind another car. You always hear drivers on the radio complaining about their tires, and this is not drama. It is data. The driver is the primary sensor for tire condition, and their feedback is a critical input to the strategy model.

The decision of when to change tires is one of the most consequential in endurance racing. Fresh tires can be worth several seconds per lap. In some conditions, three to four seconds, which over a twenty-lap stint adds up to more than a minute of race time. Changing tires costs time in the pit stop, time you might not have if the race is close. There is not just the question of when but what kind: in many racing series, teams have a choice of tire compounds, each with a different trade-off between grip and longevity. The soft tire is faster but wears out sooner, while the hard tire lasts longer but is slower. Choosing the wrong compound at the wrong time can unravel an entire race strategy.

The tire decision also interacts with every other variable. If the track temperature is climbing, the softer compound might degrade faster than expected. If rain is coming (and here is where those weather prediction models become worth their considerable investment) you might need to plan for a switch to wet-weather tires, which changes the entire pit stop sequence. If a rival team has chosen a different tire strategy, you need to model how their pace will compare to yours over the stint length. Tires are not an isolated variable. They are the variable that connects to everything else.

Car health is monitored through a combination of telemetry and driver feedback. Modern race cars are instrumented with dozens of sensors tracking engine temperature, oil pressure, brake temperatures, and suspension loads. Any of these readings drifting outside their normal range is a potential warning sign. An engine that is running hot might indicate an impending failure. Elevated brake temperatures might mean a caliper is sticking. A drop in oil pressure could mean the engine has minutes left to live. The engineer watches these indicators like a cardiologist watching an EKG, looking for the subtle deviations that precede a catastrophic event.

Driver, the most complex resource of all. In endurance racing, multiple drivers share the car, and regulations typically mandate that each driver must be in the car for a minimum amount of time. The format dictates the crew size: IMSA two-hour races require two drivers, each of whom must drive at least forty minutes. Four-hour races can have two or three drivers. The legendary twenty-four-hour races field teams of three or more drivers. I raced IMSA two-hour and four-hour races paired with Alex Prémat. I also raced the 25 Hours of Thunderhill twice with six drivers, and I have done the NASA six-hour race at Utah Motorsports Campus twice with three drivers. Each format creates a different scheduling puzzle: who drives when, for how long, and in what order?

The strategic considerations go far beyond minimum time requirements. Driver fatigue is real and progressive. Concentration degrades. Reaction times slow. Physical endurance in a car with no air conditioning, where cockpit temperatures can exceed 130 degrees, is a genuine constraint. The data coming from the car (lap times, consistency, sector times) can reveal when a driver is beginning to fade before the driver themselves recognizes it.

Then there is the question of talent. In many endurance racing formats, teams are required to field a mix of driver classifications. Some drivers are amateurs, weekend warriors who love racing and have the resources to participate, but who are measurably slower than the professionals. Others are professional drivers, often with backgrounds in single-seater racing or factory driver programs, who can extract every last tenth from the car. The strategic question of when to deploy your professional driver, early to build a lead or late to make a charge through the field, is one of the most important decisions a team makes.

The typical approach is to start with the amateur driver. Let them get their required minimum seat time in the early portion of the race when the field is still spread out and the risks of close racing are lower. Then bring in the professional for the closing stint when positions are being contested and every tenth of a second matters. This conventional wisdom is exactly that: conventional. There are situations where putting the professional in first can build an early gap that the amateur can then manage. There are situations where the amateur might actually be faster in specific conditions. Perhaps they know the track better, or their smoother driving style is better suited to wet conditions. The data helps make this decision. Historical lap time comparisons between your drivers, adjusted for conditions, give you a factual basis for what is often treated as a gut call.

All four of these resources (fuel, tires, car health, driver) are monitored continuously, their depletion rates modeled in real time, their interactions analyzed and re-analyzed as conditions change.

Boardroom Translation

A pit stop costs time in the short term but is essential to finishing the race. In business terms: a platform migration, a team reorganization, or a strategic pivot always has a transition cost. The question is not whether you can afford to stop. It is whether you can afford not to stop. The team that pits at the right moment with a clear plan loses fifteen seconds. The team that avoids the stop, but runs out of tires can lose fifteen minutes.

The Honest Truth About Real-Time

Most organizations that talk about real-time analytics are not actually doing it. They are doing near-real-time, which is perfectly respectable but not the same thing. Racing does not allow the fiction of calling hourly dashboard refreshes "real-time." The clock is running, the cars are moving, and the data is either current or it is useless.

The F1 Standard

If what I have described sounds intense, consider that it is the amateur version. Everything I have described about our pit wall operation, F1 does at a scale that is orders of magnitude larger, faster, and more sophisticated.

The Big Data in Action Mercedes-AMG GT4 racing at Portland International Raceway in the SRO GT4 Series. In a field of forty or fifty cars, the data team's job is to cut through the chaos and deliver clarity.

The Laguna Seca Gamble

There was a specific moment when all of this came together. The data, the strategy, the real-time decision-making, the resource management.

We were racing at Laguna Seca in the IMSA Michelin Pilot Challenge, October 2019. I was driving the first stint in our Mercedes-AMG GT4, holding P8, doing what a gentleman driver is supposed to do: keep the car out of trouble and in a position where the pro, my co-driver Alex Prémat, can do something with it.

Then the yellow flag came out, and strategy became everything.

Our engineer ran the numbers instantly. My tires were worn, fuel was getting low, and under green flag conditions we would have needed to pit soon. The cars ahead of me all pitted during the caution. Because we stayed out, I cycled up to P1. A gentleman driver, leading a professional field on worn tires. Terrifying.

The engineer calculated that if I could survive ten minutes after the restart, we could do it with one stop and hand off to Alex while our competitors would still need a second stop. The math worked. The tricky part was something no spreadsheet could quantify: those ten minutes on worn rubber against professional drivers on fresh tires.

He laid it out over the radio. Here is the strategy. Here is why it works. Here are the risks. What do you want to do?

I said, "Keep me out."

"Copy. Staying out. We will talk you through the restart. Conserve the fronts, protect the inside lines, do not be a hero."

As the safety car led us through Turn 11 and toward the restart zone, I was leading the entire pack. Every car behind me, thirty-four of them, was ready to pounce the moment the green flag waved. Coming around that corner, I had a fleeting thought: I should follow the safety car into the pits. It would mean two pit stops instead of one, and it would throw away the strategic advantage we had just calculated. But it would also mean I would not be heading into the Andretti Hairpin with the entire field on my bumper, every one of them on fresh tires, every one of them faster than me. For a moment, the emotional decision and the data decision were pulling in opposite directions. I stayed with the data. Whether that was courage or stubbornness, I am still not entirely sure.

This is real-time analytics in its purest form. Not a dashboard. Not a report. A human being synthesizing multiple streams of data and producing a strategic recommendation in the span of a single caution lap. No committee review. Data, judgment, and decisions. All in minutes.

The strategy was working. The math was right. The data had given us insight, and the decision-making framework had given us the courage. I will tell you how it ended in Chapter 10, and I promise it is not the ending any of us expected.

The Decision Framework

What I want you to take away from the Laguna Seca story is not the drama, though I admit the drama is part of what makes racing such an effective teaching tool. What I want you to understand is the decision framework.

At the moment that yellow flag came out, our engineer had to answer a series of questions, in order, in real time:

What is the current state of our resources? Fuel: low. Tires: degraded. Car health: good. Driver: fatigued but functional.

What are the options? Pit now during the caution or stay out and pit after the restart.

What are the consequences of each option? Pitting now means losing track position but gaining fresh tires and fuel. Staying out means maintaining position but gambling on surviving with depleted resources.

What are the competitors likely to do? Based on their observed pit stop patterns and inferred fuel/tire states, most will pit now or will need to pit shortly after the restart.

What is the net outcome of each scenario? Model the pit stop timing, the position changes, the fuel and tire deltas, and the expected finishing position under each strategy.

What is the risk tolerance? Can the driver survive two laps on degraded tires in traffic? What is the probability of an incident?

This framework – resource assessment, option identification, consequence modeling, competitive analysis, scenario comparison, risk evaluation – is not unique to racing. It is the same framework every organization should use for real-time operational decisions. The only difference is the clock speed. In racing, the entire analysis happens in two minutes. In business, you might have two hours or two days. The structure is identical.

The Gap Between Dashboards and Decisions

The war room taught me something else, something that has shaped my approach to analytics consulting ever since. There is a vast difference between displaying data and using data. The marching ants display, the lap time charts, the fuel consumption graphs. These are all beautiful visualizations. They are inert. They do not make decisions. They do not win races.

What wins races is the combination of data, domain expertise, and organizational authority to act. Our engineer had the data. He had decades of racing knowledge to interpret it. He had the authority to recommend a strategy to the driver without convening a committee. That combination – data + expertise + authority – is what transforms analytics from a spectator sport into a competitive weapon.

In too many organizations, these three elements are separated. The data team produces the data, but the domain experts do not trust it. The people with authority to act are three organizational layers removed from both. By the time the insight travels from data to expertise to authority, the moment has passed. The yellow flag is over. The race has moved on.

I have watched organizations spend tens of millions of dollars building real-time dashboards that nobody had the authority to act on. The data was current. The models were sophisticated. The insights were correct. And nothing happened because the person looking at the screen still had to send an email up three layers of management before anything could change. Imagine telling your race engineer, "Great call on the pit strategy, but let me route it through legal and get sign-off from the VP before we bring the car in." You would never finish the race. Yet that is exactly how many organizations treat their real-time data.

This is perhaps the most important lesson from the war room: real-time analytics only matters if real-time decisions are possible. And real-time decisions are only possible if your organization is structured to support them. The culture, the authority structure, the trust between the data producer and the decision-maker – these determine whether your real-time data stream is a strategic advantage or an expensive screensaver.

What Comes Next

Real-time analytics is not about speed for its own sake. It is about compressing the time between data and decision to match the tempo of the environment you are operating in. In racing, that tempo is measured in seconds. In financial markets, milliseconds. In your organization, it might be hours or days. Whatever the cadence, the data must flow to the decision-maker, and that person must have both the expertise and the authority to act at the speed of the domain. Anything less, and you are just watching the marching ants.

In the next chapter, we will see what happens when these same principles are applied with an F1 team's resources: hundreds of engineers, billions of dollars, and a data operation that makes our war room look like a lemonade stand.

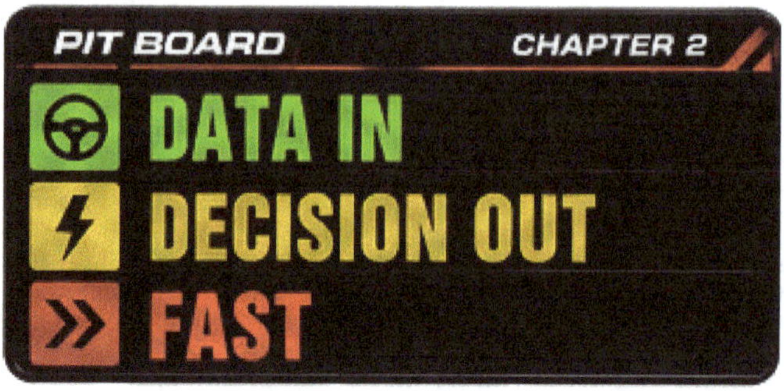

Key Lesson: The cockpit is only as good as the data that drives it. High-quality, real-time data transformed into clear insight is the fuel for better decisions.

Business Translation: Data without speed to decision creates noise, not value. Build systems that deliver the right data to the right people at the right time in the right format.

Racer Tip: Instrument what you can control, ignore what you can't. Focus on the few signals that predict performance and degradation.

Monday Action: Map the data-to-decision path for one critical decision in your organization. Remove one delay or bottleneck this week.

CHAPTER 3

Formula 1: The Pinnacle of Data-Driven Competition

How the World's Most Technologically Advanced Sport Leverages Analytics

There is a moment during every Formula 1 race weekend that most casual fans never see. During a red flag or an extended safety car period, a crew member walks onto the grid and holds a computer monitor directly in front of the driver's visor. Right there, strapped into a machine capable of 230 miles per hour, the driver studies data. Lap times. Sector splits. Tire degradation curves. Braking comparisons with their teammates. They are not waiting passively for the race to restart. They are analyzing.

Formula 1 is the most sophisticated real-time analytics operation I have ever encountered. The rest are not even close.

I have attended the United States Grand Prix at the Circuit of the Americas in Austin five or six times. The moment that crystallized it for me came during a rain-threatened race. I was standing near the pit wall when the sky darkened and the first drops began to fall. Within seconds, the energy in the pit lane changed completely. Engineers who had been calm and methodical were suddenly leaning forward, speaking rapidly into headsets, eyes darting between weather screens and timing monitors. I watched one team call their driver in for intermediate tires while the car directly behind stayed out on slicks. The team that pitted lost time while in the pit lane. The team that stayed out gained two positions, then lost four when the rain intensified two laps later and their driver was skating through corners on the wrong rubber. The entire competitive order reshuffled in the span of five minutes, and every position change was driven by a data call. Not instinct. Not tradition. A prediction model that one team trusted and the other did not have. Standing there, watching it unfold at that speed and with those stakes, I realized that what appears on television as a car race is, up close, an incredibly complex real-time analytics exercise that happens to take place at over 200 miles per hour.

You have just seen how those principles operate at the grassroots and IMSA level. This chapter is about what happens when you run them through an organization with a massive budget. Think of what follows as the existence proof: if you are wondering whether these principles scale, F1 has the answer.

A Torrent of Data at 230 MPH

Let us start with the numbers because the numbers are massive.

A modern Formula 1 car carries approximately three hundred sensors measuring everything from the obvious (speed, engine RPM, brake pressure, tire temperature) to the granular: g-forces through every corner, structural loads on the chassis, surface temperature at multiple points across each tire, hydraulic pressures in the gearbox and energy recovery systems, and airflow across dozens of points on the bodywork. All told, those three hundred sensors generate approximately 1.1 million telemetry data points per second. Over a race weekend, a single car produces terabytes of data. Multiply that by twenty-two cars on the grid, and you begin to appreciate the scale.

Raw volume is only part of the story. When a driver radios in that the car feels "loose" in the high-speed Turn 8 complex, the engineering team does not have the luxury of running a batch analysis overnight. They need answers in seconds. The cycle from sensor to insight to action typically takes less than ninety seconds.

The Architecture of Speed: F1 and the Cloud

For much of its history, Formula 1's data infrastructure was entirely local. Teams brought enormous racks of computing equipment to each race, the insights lived in the heads of engineers, and the historical knowledge walked out the door when people changed teams. That changed dramatically in 2018, when Formula 1 announced a partnership with Amazon Web Services that moved the sport's data infrastructure into the cloud. Over seventy years of historical race data (results, lap times, qualifying performances, weather conditions, pit stop records) were migrated into a unified data lake that could be queried, modeled, and analyzed at a scale that was previously impractical.

F1's cloud infrastructure now makes it possible to ask: How has the optimal pit stop window evolved over the last decade at high-degradation circuits? What weather patterns at Suzuka most frequently produce safety car periods? These are exactly the kinds of questions most businesses should be asking about their own historical data but are not, because the data is fragmented across systems that were never designed to talk to each other.

Bringing Data to the Fans: F1 Insights and Track Pulse

During broadcasts, distinct data-driven graphics, collectively known as F1 Insights, appear on screen: predictive tire performance models, real-time overtaking probability calculations factoring in DRS (Drag Reduction System) zones and historical data, and strategy simulations showing whether an early pit will pay off or cost positions.

Behind these fan-facing graphics sits a real-time analytics engine called Track Pulse. It monitors the race continuously, watching for narrative moments (pace changes, extended tire stints that suggest a strategic gamble, weather shifts that could transform the competitive order) and feeds them to the broadcast team. The result: storytelling that helps a casual viewer understand why a car running in sixth place is actually the most interesting story on the circuit.

F1 built this platform not to help teams win races but to help their customers – the fans – engage with the product. Every stakeholder in the ecosystem, whether driver, strategist, or grandstand spectator, gets data presented for their context and ability to act. That principle of contextual data delivery is one that nearly every organization needs to adopt.

Teams of Analysts, Not Just Teams of Mechanics

F1 teams have twenty or thirty people doing real-time analytics during a race. Some are trackside on the pit wall. Others sit in the team's factory thousands of miles away. When the cars are racing under floodlights in Abu Dhabi, the analytical teams at the Mercedes factory in Brackley, England, are receiving the same telemetry through the cloud, cross-referencing live data against simulation models, checking for anomalies, running strategy scenarios, and feeding recommendations back trackside.

This distributed analytics model is one of the most transferable concepts in this entire book. A regional sales manager supported by a pricing analytics team at headquarters. An ER physician supported by a radiology team reading images from another city. F1 teams have refined this model to operate in seconds rather than hours, and they have built the organizational trust that makes it work.

Boardroom Translation

F1's distributed model puts a handful of decision-makers at the point of action, backed by a much larger analytical team operating remotely. In business terms: your frontline leaders do not need to be data scientists. They need a clear radio channel to the analytical team that is doing the synthesis. The investment is not in making every manager a data expert. It is in building the communication protocols and trust that let the analysis reach the decision-maker at the speed of the decision.

The Driver as Data Consumer

F1 drivers are simultaneously data generators and data consumers. They wear biometric sensors (heart rate, core body temperature) and that data complements the car's telemetry. A spike in heart rate through a corner might indicate the rear end is unstable; elevated core temperature late in a race signals fatigue that will manifest as slower reaction times. Teams blend physiology data with vehicle dynamics to inform strategic decisions, such as whether to bring a fatiguing driver in early.

Throughout the race, the engineer feeds the driver tire temperature trends, gap data, weather forecasts, and strategy updates via radio and the steering wheel's integrated screen. During stops, a monitor is held in front of the driver so they can review braking points and sector comparisons against their teammates. This is a level of data literacy that most organizations can only dream of: frontline workers actively seeking out performance data during every pause in the action, comparing against benchmarks, looking for the tenths of a second where they could improve.

The Pit Stop Problem: Where Machine Learning Meets Strategy

Of all the strategic decisions in Formula 1, none has received more analytical attention than the pit stop. When to pit, which compound of tire to switch to, and how that decision interacts with the pit stop decisions of every other car on the circuit: this is a combinatorial optimization problem of enormous complexity that plays out in real time with incomplete information.

In a landmark collaboration, Mercedes-AMG PETRONAS partnered with researchers at Imperial College London to apply explainable reinforcement learning to the pit stop optimization problem. Using a technique called Proximal Policy Optimization, or PPO, they built a system that could evaluate the trade-offs inherent in every pit stop decision: the time lost in the pit lane versus the performance gained from fresh tires, the risk of being caught behind traffic versus the reward of running in clean air, the possibility of a safety car that could either reward or punish an early stop.

What made this work particularly important was not just the algorithm's performance but its explainability. In most machine learning applications, the model produces a recommendation but cannot articulate why. In Formula 1, where the stakes of a wrong decision are measured in millions of dollars and championship points, the engineering team needs to understand the reasoning behind a recommendation before they trust it. The Mercedes-Imperial College collaboration specifically prioritized models that could explain their logic. That is a principle every organization deploying AI should take to heart.

More recently, deep learning models applied to pit stop timing predictions have achieved 70.59 percent accuracy with 92.31 percent recall[1], numbers that were published in the context of a recent Grand Prix analysis. Those numbers might sound modest to someone accustomed to seeing accuracy figures in the high nineties for image classification or spam detection. Pit stop timing is a different kind of problem entirely. It involves predicting human decisions in a dynamic, adversarial, multi-agent environment where the optimal action depends not just on your own car's state but on the anticipated actions of the other cars, each with their own strategic imperatives. In that context, 70 percent accuracy is impressive, and the 92 percent recall figure, meaning the model catches the vast majority of optimal pit stop windows, makes it a valuable decision-support tool even if it is not infallible.

This is one of the most critical lessons for business AI. Too many organizations delay deployment because their models are not yet "accurate enough," holding them to an impossible standard while human decision-makers continue making choices with far less analytical rigor. A stakeholder asks, "What about the other thirty percent?" as though the alternative to an imperfect model is a perfect human, rather than a human guessing with a spreadsheet and gut instinct.

An F1 team does not hand the pit stop decision to the algorithm. The race strategist factors in qualitative elements the model cannot capture – the driver's radio comments, the body language of a rival team's mechanics, the instinct developed over decades – and makes the call. Human judgment plus machine intelligence consistently outperforms either one alone.

Reading the Sky: Weather as a Competitive Weapon

Weather in F1 is not a background condition. It is a strategic variable that can transform competitive order in minutes. A light drizzle arriving two laps earlier than expected can hand victory to the team that anticipated it. This is why all top teams now run their own proprietary weather prediction models, incorporating local sensor data, historical patterns at each circuit, microclimate effects, and real-time atmospheric data to produce forecasts updated continuously throughout the race.

Regulation as Design Constraint

The FIA sets technical regulations that constantly evolve, creating tension between innovation and standardization. F1 once allowed Anti-lock Braking Systems (ABS), then banned it to preserve driver skill, a direct analog to the regulatory challenges facing financial services, pharmaceuticals, and healthcare. F1 teams are masterful at innovating within boundaries: when regulations prohibit a technology, they find alternative approaches; when new rules open restricted areas, they exploit them first because they have been doing the foundational research all along. The 2026 powertrain shift, a fifty-fifty split between electric and internal combustion power, forces teams to optimize data strategies across two fundamentally different power sources, making energy deployment analytics exponentially more complex.

The Budget of Innovation

Top F1 teams operate with annual budgets in the hundreds of millions of dollars. To put it in perspective: a full season of IMSA production-based sports car racing might cost one to three million dollars. A single F1 car's annual campaign can exceed one hundred million.

But here is what I have learned: the principles scale down. You do not need three hundred sensors and thirty analysts. You need to identify your critical data streams, build the capability to turn them into insights, and deliver those insights to decision-makers fast enough to matter. Whether that means terabytes per weekend or gigabytes per quarter, the architecture is the same.

The Bridge to Your Organization

Your organization is not Formula 1. You may not have their budget, their talent density, or their single-minded focus on one measurable outcome. But you have something they do not: breadth. Your competitive landscape is far more complex than a twenty-two-car grid, which means the principles F1 has perfected – speed of insight, distributed decision support, data-literate frontline workers – create an even greater competitive advantage when applied to your environment.

In Part II, we will translate these racing principles into specific, actionable frameworks for your organization. Let's go racing.

PIT BOARD — CHAPTER 3

WIN MARGINS IN MILLIS NOT MAGIC

Key Lesson: Formula 1 shows how tiny advantages compound. Winning is not magic; it is the relentless pursuit of small gains across every system.

Business Translation: Sustainable advantage comes from optimizing the whole system, not one hero metric. Compounding 1% improvements across many areas create outsized results.

Racer Tip: Obsess over consistency and execution. The team that makes fewer small mistakes will always beat the team with more raw speed.

Monday Action: Identify one 1% improvement you can make to each step in your data value chain. Start with the easiest win.

Part II

From the Track to the Boardroom:

Five Racing Principles and Organizational Design for Your Organization

CHAPTER 4

Finding Your Ideal Corner

Principle 1: Decompose Your Key Metrics Like a Driver Decomposes a Turn

The slide on the screen showed a man in business casual, seated in an office chair, leaning forward with his hands gripping an invisible steering wheel, his face fixed with the kind of determined focus you'd expect from someone threading a car through a turn at a hundred miles an hour. The audience at the MIT CDOIQ Symposium laughed. But the image captured something important, something that sits at the heart of this chapter and, frankly, at the heart of what separates organizations that extract real competitive advantage from their data and those that merely report on what already happened.

You must figure out what your ideal corner is.

In Part I, we established that what looks simple from the grandstands – the car turns, the car accelerates – is five or six discrete sub-actions performed in precise sequence, each one influencing the next.

That insight is the foundation of the first principle: **decompose your key metrics the way a driver decomposes a turn.**

The Revenue Trap

In every role I have held, across every industry I have worked in, I have seen the same pattern. Organizations fixate on a single metric:

Revenue. Market share. Patient enrollment. Customer churn. Net Promoter Score.

They pick their number, sometimes wisely, sometimes by inertia, and they analyze the heck out of it. They build dashboards around it. They hold quarterly reviews about it. They tie compensation to it. And then they wonder why they can never seem to move it in a meaningful, sustained way.

The problem is not that they are tracking the wrong metric. The problem is that they are treating it like the intuitive driver treats a corner: as a single thing.

Revenue is not one thing. Revenue is a turn. It has a braking zone, a turn-in point, an apex, a track-out, and a straightaway exit. If you want to improve the metric rather than just report on it, you must decompose it into its constituent sub-actions and understand how each one influences the next.

Boardroom Translation

A driver does not try to "go faster." A driver brakes two meters later, releases the pedal three percent more smoothly, and gets on the throttle one car-length earlier. In business terms: stop telling your team to "improve revenue" or "reduce churn." Break the metric into its five or six sub-components, find the one with the most variance, and give your team a specific, measurable target they can act on this quarter.

Decomposing the Turn

Consider a pharmaceutical company evaluating the performance of a drug launch. The obvious metric is sales revenue in the first twelve months post-launch. Every pharmaceutical executive watches that number. Every analyst builds a model to forecast it. Every board presentation features it prominently.

Revenue from a drug launch is a corner with at least six sub-components:

The approach (braking zone): What happened in the months before launch? How effective was the medical affairs team at establishing clinical evidence and key opinion leader awareness? How many formulary decisions were secured before day one? This is the braking zone. It is where you set up everything that follows, and most organizations do not measure it with the same rigor they apply to post-launch revenue.

The turn-in point: How did the sales force ramp? Were territories aligned to where the early prescribers were concentrated? Was the messaging sharp enough to differentiate from existing therapies in the first physician conversation, or did it take three or four visits before the value proposition landed?

The apex: When did the prescription trajectory inflect? Was there a specific event (a conference presentation, a guideline update, a payer decision) that accelerated adoption? Or did the curve flatten earlier than expected because of a competitor action that nobody was monitoring?

The exit: What happened to refill rates? Were patients staying on therapy, or was the initial prescription wave masking poor adherence? What was happening in patient support programs that either reinforced or undermined the initial prescribing decision?

The following straight: What was the trajectory six months out? Were market access wins compounding, or was the launch losing momentum because the medical affairs investments had been front-loaded and then abandoned?

Each of these sub-components is measurable. Each one has leading indicators. Each one can be acted upon independently. But if you are only watching the revenue number, only watching the car go around the corner, you cannot see which sub-action is costing you time.

The same decomposition applies across industries:

	Pharma Launch	Telecom Churn	Retail Sales	Manufacturing Output
The Metric	First-year revenue	Monthly churn rate	Same-store sales	Overall equipment effectiveness
Braking Zone	Pre-launch medical affairs, formulary wins	Network quality trends, competitive offers	Foot traffic patterns, local events	Preventive maintenance schedule, supply chain lead times
Turn-In	Sales force ramp, territory alignment	Service call frequency and resolution quality	Conversion rate at point of sale	Shift changeover efficiency, operator readiness
Apex	Prescription trajectory inflection point	Customer decision moment (stay vs. switch)	Average basket size and mix	Peak throughput rate per production run
Exit	Refill rates, patient adherence	Post-resolution satisfaction, repeat contacts	Return rates, repeat visit frequency	Defect rates, rework, and scrap
Following Straight	Six-month trajectory, market access compounding	Long-term retention, lifetime value trend	Customer loyalty metrics, referral rates	Yield improvement trajectory, capacity utilization

The Leading Indicator Problem

As the speed trace comparison in Chapter 2 demonstrated, staring at the outcome metric (the 1.24-second gap) reveals nothing. Opening the telemetry and finding the specific corner where the time was lost reveals everything.

Most organizations invest most of their analytical energy on lagging indicators – metrics that tell you what already happened. Revenue last quarter. Churn last month. Patient enrollment as of yesterday. These are the equivalent of checking your lap time after you have already crossed the start-finish line. They tell you how fast you went. They do not tell you how to go faster.

The sub-components of your key metrics are leading indicators. They tell you what is about to happen and where you can intervene before the outcome is determined.

Consider a telecommunications company monitoring customer churn. The standard approach is to build a predictive churn model that identifies customers likely to leave in the next thirty or sixty or ninety days. Valuable, but the equivalent of watching your lap time and hoping it gets better. The decomposed approach asks different questions: What is the trend in customer service call frequency, and did resolutions resolve the underlying issue? What is happening with network quality in the specific geographic areas where churn is concentrated? Are customers leaving after a specific bill shock event? Has a rival launched a promotion targeting your most vulnerable segments?

Each of these sub-metrics is a section of the corner. Together, they paint a picture that the aggregate churn number simply cannot provide.

The Structured and Unstructured Insight

In Chapter 2, I described how structured telemetry data could tell us *that* we were slower through a section, but only the video – the unstructured data – could tell us *why*. The same challenge applies to every business metric.

The numbers can tell you that customer satisfaction dropped. But why? Understanding the why almost always requires qualitative, unstructured data: customer verbatims, call center transcripts, social media sentiment, field force observations.

In the pharmaceutical industry, some of the most valuable insights about drug launch performance come not from the prescription data but from the qualitative feedback captured by medical science liaisons. A physician might say, "I like the efficacy data, but I'm not comfortable with the injection device." That single sentence in a field report can explain a flattening prescription curve that no amount of structured data analysis would reveal.

You need both the speed trace and the video. Neither one alone gives you the full picture.

A Framework for Decomposition

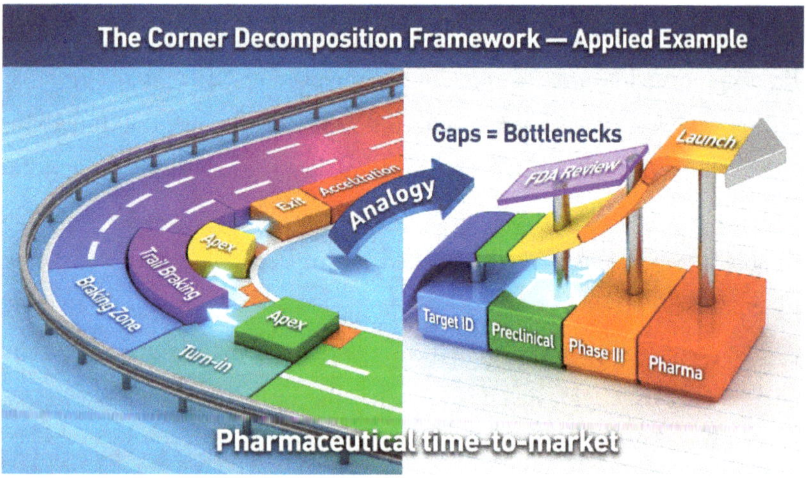

Figure 4.1: The Corner Decomposition Framework applied to pharmaceutical time-to-market, showing how a racing corner's sub-actions map directly to the stages of a drug development pipeline.

Here is a practical framework you can apply regardless of your industry. I call it the **Corner Decomposition Framework**, and it has five steps:

Step 1: Identify your critical metrics. Not all of them. Just the three to five metrics that really drive competitive advantage in your business. These are the corners that matter most on your circuit. In racing, we know that some corners matter more than others. A slow corner that leads onto a long straight has an outsized impact on lap time because any speed you lose in the corner costs you time for the entire length of the straight. Not every business metric deserves the full decomposition treatment. Focus on the ones where improvement compounds across your business.

Step 2: Map the sub-actions. For each critical metric, identify the five or six sub-components that combine to produce it. Think in terms of sequence: what happens first, what happens next, what happens after. Compare to the braking zone, the turn-in, the apex, the exit, and the following straight. What leads up to the metric? What happens during the measurement period? What happens after? Each sub-component should be something that is both measurable and actionable.

Step 3: Identify the leading indicators. For each sub-component, determine which are leading indicators and which are lagging. Leading indicators are the ones you can influence before the outcome is determined. These are your braking points, the places where a small adjustment early in the sequence produces a large change in the outcome.

Step 4: Integrate structured and unstructured data. For each sub-component, ask: what quantitative data do we have, and what qualitative data could provide the why behind the numbers? This is where you pair the speed trace with the video. This is where you combine prescription data with field force qualitative reports, or customer churn predictions with call center transcript analysis.

Step 5: Find what is unique to your business. This is perhaps the most important step. Find these items for your business because they are going to be different for every organization. The sub-components that matter for a pharmaceutical company are different from those that matter for a retailer, which are different from those that matter for an insurance company. Do not adopt someone else's decomposition wholesale. Use the framework to discover your own.

The Telecom Corner: A Deeper Look

I mentioned the telecommunications churn example briefly, but it deserves a closer look because it illustrates a subtlety that the racing analogy captures well: the relationship between sub-actions is often more important than the sub-actions themselves.

In racing, the relationship between braking and turn-in is where time is won or lost. It is not enough to brake well and turn in well independently. The transition between them must be seamless. Trail braking, the technique of gradually releasing the brake pedal while simultaneously beginning to turn the steering wheel, is what connects those two sub-actions, and it is arguably the most difficult technique in racing to master. The speed trace of a fast driver does not show a discrete "end of braking" followed by a discrete "start of turning." It shows a smooth, overlapping transition where one sub-action hands off to the next without any gap.

In telecommunications, the equivalent transition occurs between network quality and customer service. A customer who experiences a dropped call does not immediately churn. But a customer who experiences a dropped call, then calls customer service, then waits on hold for twenty minutes, then gets a resolution that does not fix the underlying issue? That customer is on the edge. The network quality problem alone is survivable. The customer service failure alone is survivable. The transition between them, the compounding of one frustration upon another, is where the relationship breaks down.

When we decomposed churn for a major telecommunications provider during my time at IBM, we discovered that the single most predictive variable was not any individual sub-metric but a specific sequence: a network quality event followed by a customer service interaction with a satisfaction score below a certain threshold, followed by a bill within fourteen days. That three-event sequence predicted churn with surprising accuracy, and it was completely invisible in the aggregate churn metric. It only became visible when we decomposed churn into its sub-components and then examined the transitions between them.

This is the equivalent of studying the trail braking zone, the transition between sub-actions, and where some of the most valuable insights live.

Why Organizations Resist Decomposition

Resistance comes from three sources. First, decomposition creates complexity – five sub-metrics are harder to communicate than one number. Second, it creates accountability – when you can see which sub-component is underperforming, someone is specifically responsible. Third, it requires different skills – decomposition is an analytical exercise, not a reporting exercise.

Start with one metric, demonstrate value, and let the results build the case. Every driver who tries the late-apex technique for the first time thinks it feels wrong. The first time you carry an extra five miles per hour onto the following straight, you are a convert.

The Pharmaceutical R&D Productivity Corner

Consider pharmaceutical R&D productivity. Most pharma companies track "time to market", the total elapsed time from initial target identification to drug approval, as a single metric. It is their ultimate KPI, reported to the board, shared with investors, scrutinized by analysts. Viewed as a single number, it reveals almost nothing actionable. It is like knowing only your total lap time without any sector splits.

Decompose that single metric into its sub-components, and the picture changes entirely: target identification to lead compound selection, preclinical testing duration, new indication filing preparation time, the gaps between Phase I, Phase II, and Phase III clinical trials, FDA review period, and commercial launch readiness. Each of these is a distinct segment of the lap, with its own braking points, apex, and exit speed.

A top ten pharmaceutical company engaged us to examine exactly this. When they decomposed their time to market, they discovered something invisible in the aggregate number: the real delays were hiding not in the phases themselves, but in the gaps between them. The technique at the heart of that discovery — analyzing the unmeasured gaps between formal process milestones rather than the milestones themselves — is the **White Space Framework**, and I will walk through it in full in Chapter 9. The short version: the solution required a calculated risk that was the pharmaceutical equivalent of carrying more speed into the corner, accepting more risk in the entry to gain on the exit.

Every element of the Corner Decomposition Framework is visible in that example. The single metric was decomposed. The leading indicator was identified. The root cause was discovered through operational analysis that went beyond the numbers. The solution required counterintuitive thinking: doing something that feels risky in the moment because the data tells you it produces a better outcome.

The Retail Corner

A large retailer I worked with was focused on same-store sales growth, a standard metric in the retail industry. They analyzed it exhaustively. They could tell you same-store sales growth by region, by store format, by product category, by week. They were treating it as one number.

When we applied the corner decomposition approach, we broke same-store sales growth into its constituent sub-actions: foot traffic (the approach), conversion rate (the turn-in), average basket size (the apex), return rate (the exit), and repeat visit frequency (the following straight). Each one had different drivers and different leading indicators.

The breakthrough came when they discovered that their conversion rate (the percentage of people who entered the store and made a purchase) was declining in a specific store format, even as foot traffic was increasing. The aggregate same-store sales number was flat, which masked the fact that they were getting more people through the door but fewer of them were buying. The structured data told them what was happening. The unstructured data told them why. Video analysis of in-store traffic patterns and customer interviews revealed a recent store layout change had inadvertently made it harder for customers to find the product categories they came in for.

That insight was invisible in the aggregate metric. It only surfaced when the metric was decomposed.

The Insurance Corner

The same pattern holds across industries. A property and casualty insurer I advised was obsessively tracking their combined ratio, the industry standard measure of underwriting profitability. They assumed their deteriorating loss ratio was driven by rising claims severity – bigger payouts per claim. That was the intuitive hypothesis, and it was wrong.

When we decomposed the combined ratio into its sub-components, the real driver was claims *frequency*, not severity, rising in a specific geographic region due to a change in weather patterns that their actuarial models had not yet incorporated. The structured data showed the deterioration. The unstructured data (adjuster field notes and weather service reports) explained the cause. Because claims frequency was a leading indicator for loss ratio, they were able to adjust their underwriting guidelines before the financial impact fully materialized. The fix was surgical, not sweeping – exactly the kind of targeted intervention that decomposition makes possible.

Getting Started: The First Corner

If the prospect of decomposing every metric in your organization feels overwhelming, here is the reassurance: you do not need to decompose every metric. You need to decompose the right ones.

Start with one. Pick the single metric that your organization talks about the most, the one that shows up in every executive meeting, the one that everyone has an opinion about, the one that has resisted improvement despite sustained attention. That metric is your Turn 1, the first corner on your circuit, the one you need to get right before you can attack the rest of the lap.

Assemble a small team, ideally a mix of business domain experts who understand the metric and analytical professionals who can structure the decomposition. Give them two weeks. Ask them to identify the five or six sub-components of that metric, determine which are leading and which are lagging, and identify one piece of unstructured data that could provide the why behind the numbers.

In my experience, the first decomposition exercise always produces at least one surprise: a sub-component that was not being measured, a leading indicator that was being ignored, a relationship between sub-actions that nobody had recognized. That surprise is your proof of concept. It is the moment where the person in the office chair stops pretending and starts actually driving.

The Chair and the Steering Wheel

I come back to that image from the presentation. The person in the office chair, gripping an invisible steering wheel, leaning into an invisible corner. It is funny. It is also exactly right.

The principles that make a race car driver fast are the principles that make an organization fast. You cannot improve your performance by staring at the outcome. You improve your performance by breaking the outcome into its sub-actions, measuring each one independently, understanding the relationship between them, and finding the specific sub-action where improvement will have the greatest impact.

Every industry has its ideal corners. In pharmaceuticals, it might be the drug launch curve. In telecommunications, the customer lifecycle from acquisition through retention. In retail, the same-store sales equation. In insurance, the combined ratio. In financial services, customer lifetime value. In manufacturing, overall equipment effectiveness. Every one of these is a corner, not a straightaway. Every one of them can be decomposed. Every one of them is hiding insights in its sub-components that the aggregate number obscures.

Find your ideal corner. Decompose it. And then find where you are losing time.

Key Lesson: Every organization has an ideal way to use data. It is the path that maximizes value while fitting your strategy, capabilities, and culture.

Business Translation: Stop chasing someone else's data strategy. The right approach is the one that fits your roadmap and resources.

Racer Tip: Know your track. Play to your strengths, and be honest about your weak corners.

Monday Action: Define what success looks like for your data program in 12 months given your organization's strategy and constraints.

CHAPTER 5

Managing Your Pit Crew

Principle 2: Predict and Monitor Your Key Resources, Not Just Your Outcomes

Thirty minutes into a two-hour endurance race, I am focused on hitting my marks: braking at the crack in the pavement before Turn 2, carrying speed through Turn 7, feeding the throttle smoothly onto the front straight. But behind the pit wall, my engineer is watching something entirely different. He is not watching my lap time. He is watching my resources.

How much fuel is left in the tank? At the current consumption rate, how many more laps before we have to pit? What are the tire temperatures? The right front has been climbing steadily for the last eight laps. Is it approaching the threshold where grip will fall off a cliff, or can we push it for another stint? What about the driver? Am I making more mistakes than I was twenty minutes ago? Are my lap times degrading in a pattern that suggests fatigue rather than traffic?

These are not outcome questions. These are resource questions. They are hugely important in a racing program.

This distinction, between predicting outcomes and predicting resources, is the second principle I want you to take from the racetrack to your organization. Most organizations get this wrong, and the consequences are more severe than most leaders realize.

The Four Resources That Win Races

In Chapter 2, I introduced the four critical resources that drive every strategic decision in endurance racing: fuel, tires, car health, and the driver. The Laguna Seca gamble illustrates what happens when multiple resources deplete simultaneously. My tires were shot. I was fatigued. The stress of restarting in traffic compounded everything. The outcome was the product of multiple resources being depleted at once, each one compounding the effect of the others.

The Business Parallel

Most companies I have worked with are reasonably good at predicting business outcomes. They build forecasting models for revenue, market share, customer acquisition, patient enrollment. Very few predict and monitor the resources that produce those outcomes.

Within a business, each organization has to figure out what its key resources are: human resources (data scientists, curators, analysts), infrastructure resources (pipelines, data volumes, processing capacity), and what I call decision resources – the number of decisions actually being made based on the analytics being produced. If any one of them runs dry, the outcome suffers regardless of how good your outcome prediction model is.

Boardroom Translation

A racing team constantly monitors fuel, tires, vehicle health, and driver endurance because exhausting any one of them ends the race. Data programs operate the same way. Your budget, team capacity, technology infrastructure, and executive sponsorship are the resources that sustain progress. Most leaders track only the budget. But the resource that runs out first is the one that ends the program—and it's usually not the budget.

Running Out of Fuel Mid-Project

Here is a pattern I have seen more times than I care to count. An organization launches an ambitious data and analytics initiative. The business case is sound. Executive sponsorship is strong. The project kicks off with energy and optimism.

Six months in, the project stalls. Not because the business case was wrong, but because the organization ran out of fuel. Sometimes the fuel is people – three of twelve data engineers pulled onto another initiative, the remaining nine burning out. Sometimes the fuel is data – integration work behind schedule because data quality was worse than anyone expected. Sometimes the fuel is attention – the executive sponsor who championed the project got promoted or reassigned.

In every case, the organization predicted the outcome but did not predict the resources required to get there. They were watching the lap time and assuming the car would keep running.

According to industry analysis, eighty-five percent of big data projects fail to deliver on their objectives[2]. That statistic would be unacceptable in any racing program.

Companies with strong data integration and literacy are about six times more likely to achieve significant financial benefits from AI than organizations with poor connectivity and skills[3]. It is the difference between putting a trained professional driver in the car versus someone who has never turned a wheel in anger.

I call this the **fuel gauge fallacy**. Organizations assume that because they planned for the resources at the start, those resources will remain available throughout the project's life. They set the fuel load and stop checking the gauge. In racing, no engineer would fill the tank at the start and stop monitoring consumption. Yet the typical project plan says we need fifteen data engineers for eighteen months, hires them, checks the box, and never rechecks. Six months later, three have been reassigned, two have resigned, and the remaining ten are working on scope that has grown by forty percent.

The Pit Stop Decision Framework

In practice, the pit stop is the moment where resource predictions translate into action. The engineer has been monitoring fuel, tires, car, and driver for the entire stint. Now the car comes into the pits, and a series of decisions must be made in seconds:

Do we change tires? If so, all four, or just the ones that are worn? What compound do we switch to? The softer tire is faster but degrades more quickly, so is there enough race left to justify it? How much fuel do we add? Fill the tank for the rest of the race, or add just enough for the next stint to keep the car light? Do we change the driver? If the current driver is fatigued, putting in a fresh driver might gain us a second per lap. But the driver change takes additional time in the pits. Is the net gain worth the pit lane time? Is anything wrong with the car? If the brakes are overheating, do we spend fifteen seconds adjusting the brake bias, or do we send the car out and manage it with driving technique?

Every one of these decisions is a resource allocation decision, made based on predictive models: tire degradation, fuel consumption, driver performance curves, and mechanical wear rates.

Now apply this framework to your organization.

The tire decision: Your data scientists have been working at an unsustainable pace for three months. Output quality is starting to degrade. Models are taking longer to validate, documentation is getting thinner, testing is being shortcut. Do you push them for another sprint, or do you bring in reinforcements (change the tires) even though the transition will cost you a few weeks of productivity while the new people ramp up?

The fuel decision: Your data infrastructure budget is being consumed faster than planned because the data volumes are larger than anticipated and the cloud computing costs are higher. Do you request more budget now (add fuel), or do you try to optimize consumption and stretch what you have? If you wait too long, you run dry in the middle of a critical deliverable.

The driver decision: Your project leader has been running this initiative for eighteen months. They know it intimately, but they are showing signs of fatigue: slower decision-making, less engagement with stakeholders, a tendency to defer difficult conversations. Do you rotate in new leadership, accepting the short-term disruption of a handoff, or do you keep the current leader in the seat and hope they recover?

The car decision: Your data platform is showing signs of strain. Query performance is degrading. Jobs that used to run in two hours now take four. The architecture that was designed for your initial data volumes is struggling with the scale you have reached. Do you invest in re-architecture now, a significant effort that will slow visible progress for months, or do you keep running and hope the platform holds together long enough to deliver the current phase?

These are pit stop decisions. And they can only be made well if you have been monitoring your resources all along.

Building a Resource Prediction Capability

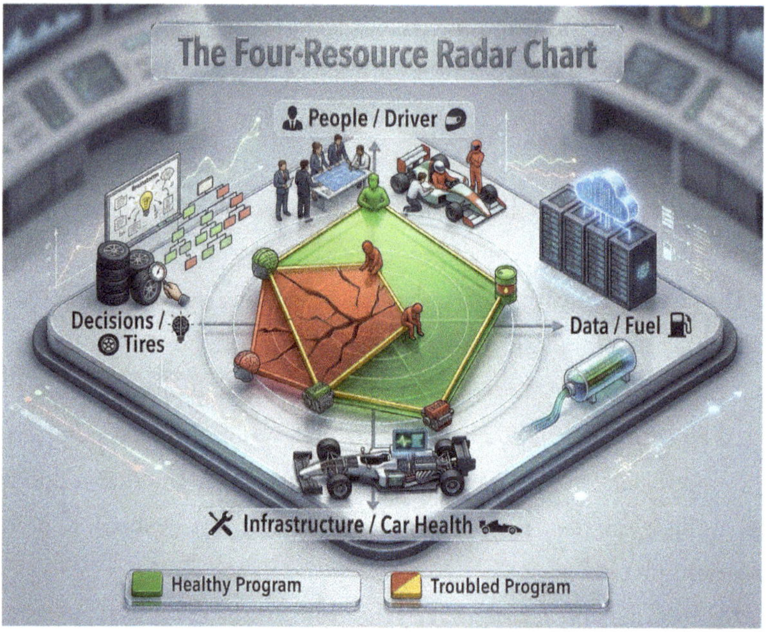

Figure 5.1: The Four-Resource Radar Chart showing a healthy, balanced data program versus one heading for trouble, mapped to the racing equivalents of fuel, tires, car health, and driver.

Far fewer organizations have an equivalent capability for predicting resource utilization. Here is what building that capability looks like:

Identify your four resources. For most data and analytics programs, these fall into four areas:

People resources: The number and availability of key roles: data scientists, data engineers, data stewards, analysts, project managers. Not just headcount, but effective capacity. A data scientist split across three projects is not the same resource as one who is fully dedicated. Track not just how many people you have, but how much of their capacity is actually available for the work that matters.

Data resources: The availability, quality, and readiness of the data assets your program depends on. How much of the data you need has been acquired? How much has been integrated? How much has been validated for quality? Data readiness is the equivalent of fuel. If you run out, everything stops.

Infrastructure resources: The capacity and performance of your computing environment, your data storage, your processing pipelines, your analytical tools. Infrastructure that was sized for last year's data volumes may be inadequate for this year's. Monitor utilization trends and model when you will hit capacity constraints.

Decision resources: This one is less intuitive but critically important. Are the decisions that your analytics were designed to support actually being made? Are decision-makers consuming the insights you are producing? If you are generating analytical output that nobody is acting on, you have a decision resource problem. You have plenty of fuel but no one is pressing the accelerator.

Build predictive models for each resource category. This does not have to be sophisticated. A simple trend model that projects when you will run out of data engineer capacity is far more valuable than no model at all. In racing, the engineer's fuel calculation is displayed on the screen in real time. Your resource projections should be equally transparent.

Monitor leading indicators of resource degradation. Just as tire temperatures predict tire failure before it happens, there are leading indicators for each resource. For people: increasing overtime, rising turnover, declining output quality. For data: growing quality exception rates and expanding onboarding timelines. For infrastructure: rising query times and increasing job failures. For decisions: declining consumption of analytical outputs.

Create a pit board. In racing, the pit board is a physical sign the team holds out as the car passes each lap – position, gap, instructions. Concise and impossible to miss. Your data program needs the same: a single view showing people capacity, data readiness, infrastructure headroom, and decision adoption. Reviewed weekly. Visible to the entire team.

The Compounding Effect of Resource Depletion

Resource depletion is nonlinear. A fatigued driver on worn tires is not just slower by the sum of both issues – the combination is multiplicative. A tired driver is less able to compensate for reduced grip, which leads to more mistakes, which accelerates fatigue further and can lead to disaster.

The same dynamic occurs in data programs. Fewer people means less capacity for data quality remediation, which means more workarounds, slower progress, more pressure, higher turnover, resulting in even fewer people. By the time compounding becomes visible in your outcome metrics, the underlying depletion is already severe. The time to act was twenty laps ago.

The Outcome-Resource Disconnect

Organizations predict destinations with great sophistication but predict fuel supply with a back-of-the-envelope estimate. It does not matter how good your race strategy is if you run out of fuel on lap forty-two.

I know this firsthand. At the 2018 IMSA race at Virginia International Raceway, we had been running a strong race but needed a splash of fuel to make it to the finish. Alex was in the car and brought it into the pits for a quick stop. Every second the car sits in the box, the competition is gaining ground or passing outright, so the calculus is brutal. Our engineer calculated that thirty seconds of fueling would get us to the end. Alex stopped, the crew connected the fuel hose, and the engineer watched the clock. At thirty seconds, he called to release the car, and Alex was back on track.

He drove brilliantly, working Car 92 up into the top ten as the race approached its final laps. Then, on the last lap, the engine stumbled and went silent in Turn 2. Out of fuel. Alex coasted to a stop with the finish line tantalizingly close. A few more seconds on the fuel hose would have gotten us there, but those same seconds would have cost us positions to the cars behind us. We lost the gamble.

There is an adage in project management: you can have it good, cheap, or fast, pick two. Racing has its own version: fuel, time, and position. Fill the tank and you finish the race, but you lose track position while your competitors drive past an empty pit stall. Take a short stop and keep your position, but you might not have enough fuel to reach the checkered flag. Math is unforgiving, and so is the clock.

A Tale of Two Programs

Consider two data programs I observed, one that monitored its resources and one that did not.

The first was a large financial services firm building a customer analytics platform. Strong business case, talented team, solid executive sponsorship. They did not monitor their resources. Weekly status meetings focused entirely on deliverables and milestones.

Eight months in, three things happened simultaneously.

Their lead data architect – the one person who held the complete mental model of the platform in his head – accepted a position at a competitor. Critical design decisions had never been documented. Integration patterns existed only in his memory.

Before the team recovered, their primary data source was migrated to a new platform by the source system team on a timeline the analytics group had not been consulted on. Half of the integration pipelines broke silently, producing data that looked correct but carried subtle errors that took weeks to detect.

Then a corporate budget review cut their cloud infrastructure allocation by twenty percent, forcing the team to simultaneously fight fires and reduce their capacity to fight them.

Any one of these events was manageable alone. Together, they were catastrophic – the organizational equivalent of a tire failure triggering a spin that collects two other cars. The twelve-month program delivered in twenty months, at twice the budget, with reduced scope. The team's morale never fully recovered.

The second program was a different story. A pharmaceutical company building a real-world evidence analytics capability. From the outset, the program leader instituted a "resource radar" – every two weeks, the team reviewed effective people capacity, data readiness, infrastructure headroom, and decision adoption.

Four months in, the radar flagged a problem: data readiness was falling behind. Three external data sources took longer to integrate than expected. In the first program, this would have been discovered when someone tried to build a model and found the data missing. In the second, it was detected early enough to adjust. The team reallocated engineers and negotiated extensions. The program stayed on track because the resource problem was detected before it cascaded.

The difference was not talent, budget, or executive support. One team monitored their resources. The other did not.

Bringing It Together

The fastest car in the field cannot win if it runs out of fuel.

Consider a manufacturing plant running 24/7 production. The four-resource framework maps directly: raw materials and energy are the fuel (predictable depletion, catastrophic if you run out). Equipment wear is the tire degradation (nonlinear; a machine does not slowly degrade and then politely stop; it performs adequately until a bearing fails and takes out an entire production line). The plant infrastructure, HVAC, electrical, compressed air, is the car's mechanical health (cumulative stress that requires monitoring, not just reaction). And operator fatigue across shifts is the driver, the human variable that determines whether all the other resources are used well or wasted. Organizations that monitor only output, the equivalent of watching only lap time, miss the resource degradation that precedes every unplanned shutdown.

In the next chapter, we will turn from predicting resources to organizing the people who deliver them – and I will share the organizational model that made the biggest difference in my career.

Key Lesson: Winning teams have the right people in the right roles, working together toward a shared objective.

Business Translation: Data programs fail when roles are unclear, skills are missing, or egos create friction. Clarity in roles and trust in the team drive performance.

Racer Tip: Respect every role. From the driver to the mechanic, every position touches performance.

Monday Action: Review your data team's roles and responsibilities. Clarify one role that is causing confusion.

CHAPTER 6

Building the Pit Crew: Organizational Design for Data Programs

Structuring the Team That Turns Data Into Decisions

The Human Resource as the Most Critical Variable

I want to spend a moment on the most important and most neglected resource: people.

In endurance racing, the driver is unique among the four resources because the driver is the one resource that is both self-aware and self-regulating. Fuel does not know it is running low. Tires do not know they are worn. The driver knows they are tired. This creates a peculiar problem. Drivers, like data professionals, tend to underreport their own degradation. They do not want to be seen as the limiting factor. They want to stay in the car. They push through fatigue because they are competitive, because they are committed, because they believe they can manage it.

Your most talented data scientists will work nights and weekends to deliver a model on time. Your most dedicated data engineers will absorb the impact of scope creep and changing requirements without complaint. They will not tell you they are exhausted until they are so far past the point of diminishing returns that their output is becoming counterproductive, introducing errors, and making poor architectural decisions.

The engineer behind the pit wall monitors the driver's performance objectively. Looking for the telltale signs of fatigue that the driver may not recognize or may not admit, such as increasing lap time variability, inconsistency in braking points, and more frequent corrections after corner entry. The data is more honest than the driver's self-report.

You need to do the same for your team. Monitor the objective indicators of team health (quality metrics, velocity trends, defect rates, cycle times) and use them to make resource decisions before your people burn out. The most expensive mistake in any data program is losing a critical team member to burnout. The replacement cost in time and lost knowledge is enormous. It is the equivalent of destroying an engine because you ignore the temperature gauge. This is also, fundamentally, a culture question. A team that does not trust the data enough to act on it is depleted regardless of headcount. A culture that treats people as interchangeable resources rather than the most critical variable in the system will burn through talent faster than it can be replaced.

Building the Pit Crew: The Center of Excellence Model

The racing analogy extends naturally to how you organize the people who support the program. In racing, the pit crew is not a random collection of mechanics. It is a carefully structured team with defined roles and practiced coordination. The same principle applies to building a data and analytics organization.

At GlaxoSmithKline, I built the Center of Excellence for data from the ground up. It started as a tiger team of about twenty people in the first year, laser-focused on standing up the initial platform and delivering the first business use cases. Over four years, it grew to approximately one hundred people organized around three pillars.

The first pillar was Data Build, the team responsible for designing and delivering the platform and the tools to support the entire program. These were the architects, the engineers, the infrastructure specialists who kept the race car running.

The second pillar was Data Use, and this is where the translator model lived. Data Use was comprised of three teams: Domain Services, which focused on organizing source data into coherent groups of related information; Data Science, which worked directly with the business on what I always called the "art of the possible" in the use of the data; and Data Enablement and Adoption, which helped the business develop use cases that would drive tangible value to the organization.

The third pillar was Data Strategy, providing oversight and governance to ensure consistency across the entire program.

The most critical hires in the entire organization were the translators, the people I think of as "scientists with a data problem." They were recruited from across the R&D organization. They were the recognized data leaders in their respective areas, the people everyone already went to when they needed to find data about a chemical compound or locate experiments done ten years ago on a particular drug discovery. We hired chemists and biologists who also had deep experience in data. They could speak both languages. They understood the science at a molecular level and they understood data architecture, curation, and analytics. Scientists naturally gravitate toward working with people who share their background and can speak their language. These translators bridged the gap between the scientific disciplines and the data engineering required to organize information for maximum value.

Rather than trying to turn every scientist into a data engineer or every data engineer into a scientist, you create a layer of people fluent in both worlds. They are the engineer behind the pit wall – the person who understands both the driver's experience and the telemetry data. Without that translator, the driver and the data are speaking different languages.

The model is not unique to pharmaceuticals. At IBM, I saw it work in financial services (translators were actuaries who understood both risk mathematics and data engineering) and telecommunications (translators were network engineers who understood both RF propagation and data architecture). The title changes. The principle is universal.

Boardroom Translation

A racing team's pit crew is not a random collection of mechanics — it is a carefully structured unit with defined roles and rehearsed coordination. The translator model applies the same principle to data organizations: rather than expecting scientists to become data engineers or data engineers to become scientists, you create a bridge role fluent in both worlds. The organizations that solve this translation problem are the ones whose data investments reach the people making decisions.

How We Found Them: Recruiting Translators

My approach when joining any new organization is to have structured discussions with as many leaders as possible to understand the current state of data and analytics. At GSK, I started with my boss, the President of R&D, and then moved systematically to all his direct reports. I kept a common structure for these conversations so I could organize the responses into coherent action plans. One question I always asked was deceptively simple: "Who do you go to when you have a question that requires data or analytics?"

At the senior level, the answer was usually a manager or director who led a department — computational chemistry, clinical development, biostatistics. But as I worked my way deeper into the organization, the answers changed. They became personal. "Oh, I always go to Sarah. She is the only one who knows how to extract data from the system." Or: "Well, to be honest, Joe has built an Excel spreadsheet that lets us quickly sort out questions about manufacturing defects."

Every organization has these people. They are the informal business analysts who have figured out how to break down the barriers across data silos and get to the gold. They are the ones their colleagues rely on to find the data needed to finish a project or answer a question. They have earned that role not through a job title but through a combination of domain expertise and data fluency that makes them indispensable within their teams.

The challenge with this situation is that it does not scale. Sarah and Joe can serve a department of fifty people, but there are never enough of them to impact every department. Their knowledge is local. Their solutions are bespoke. The Excel spreadsheet that sorts out manufacturing defect questions is brilliant within its scope, but it does not connect to the clinical data that would make the insight three times more valuable.

By identifying these individuals and bringing them into the Center of Excellence, we could leverage their talents at a broader level and unlock the data for use by more of their colleagues. These were our translators. We did not recruit from outside the organization or post job descriptions on career sites. We found them by listening, by asking the same questions at every level of the organization, and by paying attention to the names that kept coming up. The best translators were already doing the work. They just did not have the title, the tools, or the organizational mandate to do it at scale.

Measuring What Matters: The Impact of the Translator Model

You can build the most elegant architecture in the industry, load every data source, and deliver dashboards that would make an F1 team's engineering staff jealous. None of it matters if the scientists do not use it.

Getting business users to adopt a new approach is difficult. Getting them to discontinue the old approach is even harder. Scientists are busy. They have familiar tools that work well enough. The short-term friction of change is concrete while the long-term benefit is abstract.

The translators were the key. Because they came from the business, they could bridge the adoption gap in a way that no data engineer or project manager could. A translator could sit with a research team, understand what they were trying to accomplish, and show them how the new platform made that specific task faster. Not a demo of features. A demonstration of value, delivered in the language of the scientist's own work.

The key metric was platform adoption. Were scientists using the new system? More importantly, were we able to turn off the old data flows? The translators' job was to make the new platform not just available but indispensable.

When the Model Breaks: Failure Modes and Lessons Learned

The translator approach was highly successful. But it was not without failure modes, and understanding those failures is as important as understanding the successes.

The most common failure pattern was what I think of as the small-pond problem. Some translators thrived when they were the go-to data person in a department of fifty people. They were the big fish in a small pond, and that status drove their performance. They loved being the one everyone relied on. They took pride in knowing every corner of their department's data landscape. When we brought them into the Center of Excellence and asked them to operate at a broader level, serving hundreds of users across multiple departments, that recognition faded. The pressure to perform in a visible, local way was replaced by a more diffuse mandate, and some translators lost the drive that had made them exceptional in the first place.

It was like taking a club racer who dominates their local series and putting them in a national championship. The skills are the same. The car is the same. But the context has changed, and some drivers are energized by the bigger stage while others are diminished by it. You cannot always predict which way it will go until you see them in the new environment.

The related failure mode was the inability to let go. Some translators remained emotionally and operationally tethered to their previous department. They continued to prioritize requests from their old colleagues over the broader needs of the organization. They could not make the transition from serving fifty people they knew personally to serving five hundred they did not. Their loyalty, which had been a strength in the departmental context, became a limitation in the enterprise context.

In racing terms, it is the driver who is fast on their home track but cannot adapt to a circuit they have never seen. The fundamental talent is there, but the ability to generalize, to apply the same skills in an unfamiliar environment, is a separate capability that not everyone possesses.

If I were building the model again, I would invest more in the transition itself. We moved people into the Center of Excellence and expected them to adapt. What we should have done is create a more deliberate onboarding process that acknowledged the identity shift involved. Being the data person in a department is a personal role. Being a translator in an enterprise data organization is a professional role. Those are different things, and the transition between them deserves the same structured support that any significant role change requires.

Key Lesson: A great data program is intentionally designed with the right structure, talent, processes, and governance.

Business Translation: Structure follows strategy. Design your organization to accelerate decisions and adapt as the business evolves.

Racer Tip: Build for speed and flexibility. Over-engineering will slow you down in the long run.

Monday Action: Make one structural change that will improve collaboration or speed in your data organization.

CHAPTER 7

Beyond the Track Walls

Principle 3: Expand the Use of External Data for Tactical and Strategic Decisions

A note on scope before we get to the weather. This chapter is about the external data your industry already knows exists – the academic literature, regulatory filings, licensed commercial feeds, and public records that every serious competitor can access. The competitive question is not whether to use it, but whether you integrate it better and push it deeper into tactical decisions than the rest of your industry does. Chapter 8 takes up the harder, separate problem: finding data your industry does not yet know exists for it at all.

It is 6:00 a.m. on race day. The sky is overcast, a cloud layer is building, and our entire race strategy is about to be determined by data that has nothing to do with our car.

The question is: is it going to rain?

Not just whether it will rain, but how much. When will it start? When will it stop? Whether it will be a drizzle that makes the track greasy but does not justify switching to rain tires, or a downpour that turns the racing surface into a skating rink and changes the competitive order entirely.

Top racing teams do not rely on the Weather Channel app. They build or acquire their own meteorological models, tailored to the specific microclimate of the track, updated in near-real-time with data from portable weather stations around the circuit. If you know rain will arrive in twenty minutes, you can pit now for rain tires before the rest of the field. If you know the rain will be brief, you might stay out on dry tires and avoid an extra stop while others pit twice.

That investment in external data is what separates organizations that merely report on their business from organizations that shape it.

Boardroom Translation

Every F1 team gets the same public weather forecast. The ones that win build their own models. In business terms: if your competitive intelligence comes from the same industry reports, analyst briefings, and vendor dashboards that every competitor reads, you do not have competitive intelligence. You have shared knowledge. The advantage comes from data sources your competitors have not thought to acquire.

The 80 Percent Problem

Here is a number that surprises everyone I share it with. In my experience at GSK and with other pharmaceutical organizations, approximately eighty percent of the data used for R&D decisions originated from external sources. The logic is straightforward: even a large pharmaceutical company performs only a tiny fraction of global research. That external data is academic research, competitor clinical trial data, real-world evidence from electronic health records, genomic data from public repositories, regulatory guidance, and epidemiological data from public health agencies.

On top of that, eighty percent of that external data is unstructured or semi-structured – buried in PDFs, embedded in research papers, scattered across websites, hidden in the free-text fields of regulatory submissions.

The FDA underscored this reality in December 2024 by launching a new CDER Center for Real-World Evidence Innovation. External control arms, where historical external patient data substitutes for a traditional placebo group, are becoming mainstream, particularly in oncology and rare diseases where randomized trials are impractical or unethical.

The pharmaceutical industry may be the most extreme example, but the pattern holds across industries. The data that describes your competitive ecosystem overwhelmingly originates outside your own systems.

The Strategic-to-Tactical Shift

Most organizations use external data exclusively for strategic purposes: board-level decisions, annual planning, five-year strategy. What they should be doing is pushing it all the way down to tactical and operational decision-making.

Consider the difference in racing. The strategic use of weather data is deciding which races to enter based on historical patterns. The tactical use is making pit stop decisions during the race itself. Both are valuable. But tactical use is where the competitive advantage lives because everyone has access to the same strategic information.

Every pharmaceutical company subscribes to the same IQVIA market data. Every consumer goods company has Nielsen. At the strategic level, external data is a commodity. The advantage comes when you push it down to tactical decisions – when the pharmaceutical company adjusts enrollment strategies based on what competitors are doing this month, when the retailer moves seasonal inventory between stores based on seventy-two-hour temperature forecasts, when the insurer routes adjusters to the hardest-hit areas within hours using satellite imagery.

Most organizations are not doing this.

The After-the-Fact Mastering Problem

There is a reason most organizations struggle with external data, and it is a deeply practical one. When you generate data internally, you control its format, its schema, and its governance. You define the data model. You enforce the naming conventions. You decide how missing values are handled. You own it.

External data arrives on someone else's terms.

During the MIT CDOIQ Symposium where I presented, Dr. Michael Stonebraker, one of the most influential database researchers in history and a Turing Award laureate, introduced a concept that has profoundly shaped how I think about external data. He called it "after-the-fact mastering." Stonebraker did not just theorize about this problem. He founded Tamr, an AI-driven data mastering company, to put this philosophy into practice at enterprise scale.

The insight is clean in its simplicity: with eighty percent of your data coming in externally, you have no control over it. You did not design the schema. You did not define the data quality rules. You did not choose the field formats or the code tables or the temporal granularity. The data arrives the way it arrives, and it is different from every source, and it is inconsistent in ways that would make a data architect weep.

So, what you must do is bring it in and make it look the way you would like it to look if you had control over it from the beginning. You master it after the fact.

This is a very different philosophy from the traditional approach to data management, which emphasizes upfront modeling, rigid schemas, and comprehensive data governance established before the first record is loaded. That traditional approach works beautifully for internal data, where you control the source systems. It fails catastrophically for external data, because you cannot impose your standards on academic journals, government databases, competitor websites, social media platforms, or third-party data providers.

Forget about the fact of trying to mandate that upfront, because it has failed for twenty years and it is not going to work now. Dr. Stonebraker was blunt about this, and he was right. The organizations that have tried to apply traditional upfront data governance to external data have spent years building elaborate data models and integration frameworks that are obsolete before they are completed, because the external sources changed, or new sources became available, or the business requirements shifted.

After-the-fact mastering accepts chaos. It says: bring the data in as it arrives. Store it in its native form. And then apply mastering, harmonization, and governance as a downstream process, one that can be iterative and adaptive.

This approach requires different technology and different organizational thinking. But it is the only approach that scales to the volume and variety of external data that modern organizations need to consume.

The GSK Experience

An experience from my time as Chief Data and Analytics Officer at GlaxoSmithKline illustrates both the opportunity and the challenge of external data at scale.

At GSK, I led the development of the R&D Information Platform, which we called RDIP. This was a massive undertaking: nearly two thousand nodes, over forty petabytes of storage, built on Cloudera. The platform consolidated structured and unstructured data across the organization into a shared platform for AI/ML, analytics, search, and reporting. RDIP delivered genome-wide association studies (GWAS) on UK Biobank and 23andMe data, standardized assay data, standardized clinical trial data, and consolidated portfolio data for R&D.

The reason the platform had to be that large was not primarily because of GSK's internal data. GSK generated significant internal data, to be sure: clinical trial data, laboratory data, manufacturing data, commercial data.

But the platform's scale was driven by the external data requirement. To support drug discovery and development decisions, GSK's scientists and analysts needed access to the vast universe of external biomedical data. That meant genomic databases, published literature, patent filings, regulatory submissions, real-world evidence, epidemiological datasets, and dozens of other external sources.

The hard part was the mastering – making external genomic data interoperable with internal clinical trial data, harmonizing terminology across decades of published literature, reconciling real-world evidence with clinical trial endpoints.

This is where Stonebraker's philosophy proved essential. We could not wait until all external data was perfectly harmonized. The competitive clock was ticking. So, we brought the data in, stored it in its native form, and built iterative mastering pipelines that progressively harmonized it. Scientists could access the raw data immediately and the mastered data as it became available. Imperfect but accessible data today was worth far more than perfectly harmonized data eighteen months from now.

This is why industry standard data models are critical. An organization's clinical trial data from the past will not all be in a consistent format. But by loading first and then standardizing into the CDISC standard (the Clinical Data Interchange Standards Consortium format used across the pharmaceutical industry), the data could be shared in a consistent, queryable format. Load first, harmonize after – across every data domain.

Types of External Data

Most organizations focus almost exclusively on the data they generate internally. Yet many of the signals that explain customer behavior, market shifts, competitive threats, and operational risks originate outside the organization. External data expands your field of view, providing context that internal data alone cannot.

The good news is that external data is more accessible than ever. Some sources are freely available, others are available for purchase, and many can be obtained through partnerships. The challenge is rarely access—it is recognizing which external signals can improve decisions and integrating them into the way the organization operates.

Published and public data: academic research, government statistics, regulatory filings, patent databases. Abundant, often free, and frequently overlooked.

Licensed commercial data: market research, competitive intelligence, economic indicators, consumer panel data. Most organizations already subscribe for strategic purposes. The opportunity is to push it into tactical decision-making.

Partner and ecosystem data: supply chain data, channel partner data, collaborative research programs. Often available but underleveraged because no one has asked.

Real-time environmental data: weather, traffic, satellite imagery, social media, event data. Most valuable for tactical decisions – the decisions that happen in the moment.

Alternative data: satellite imagery of parking lots, shipping container tracking, job posting data, app download statistics. Valuable exactly because your competitors may not be using them.

The Cultural Shift

Many organizations believe internal data is trustworthy and external data is suspect. The reality: internal data is not as clean as most organizations believe, and external data is not as dirty as they fear. Our racing weather models were wrong sometimes, but they were right more often than guessing. Perfect was not the standard. Better than the alternative was the standard.

Practical Steps for Implementation

If you are a data leader looking to expand your organization's use of external data, here is a practical roadmap:

Step 1: Audit your decision landscape. Identify the twenty most important decisions your organization makes, from strategic (which markets to enter) to tactical (which customers to target this week). For each decision, inventory the data that currently informs it. Then ask: what external data could improve this decision? You will find that for most decisions, there is external data available that is not being used.

Step 2: Start with the tactical. I know this seems counterintuitive. Most organizations start with strategic external data because it feels safer and more manageable. But the competitive advantage of external data is largest at the tactical level, where decisions are made frequently and the feedback loop is short. Start with a tactical use case where you can demonstrate value quickly.

Step 3: Build an external data acquisition capability. This is a capability, not a project. It includes the ability to discover relevant external data sources, negotiate access (whether through purchase, partnership, or public access), ingest data in its native format, and make it available for analysis. This capability should be persistent, always scanning for new sources, always evaluating the quality and relevance of existing sources, always adapting to changes in the external data landscape.

Step 4: Adopt after-the-fact mastering. Do not try to harmonize all external data before making it available. Bring it in, store it natively, and build iterative mastering pipelines that progressively improve quality and interoperability. Accept that some external data will always be messy. The alternative, waiting until it is perfect, means waiting forever.

Step 5: Govern differently. External data cannot be governed the same way you govern internal data. You do not control the source, the schema, the update frequency, or the quality. Your governance framework for external data needs to focus on fitness for purpose, provenance tracking, update monitoring, and usage guidelines rather than source-level quality enforcement. Build metadata that captures where the data came from, when it was acquired, what transformations have been applied, and what its known limitations are.

Step 6: Build trust through demonstration. The best way to overcome cultural resistance to external data is to demonstrate its value. Find an area where external data produces a measurably better outcome, document it rigorously, and share the story broadly. One strong success story does more to shift culture than a hundred strategy decks.

After-the-Fact Mastering in Practice

Consider a pharmaceutical company integrating three thousand published research papers. The traditional approach: define a comprehensive data model upfront, hire curators, spend months producing a dataset that is immediately incomplete because new papers are published every week. The after-the-fact approach: ingest all three thousand papers in their native form. Apply NLP to extract entities and relationships – drug names, disease names, dosages, outcomes – without requiring a predefined schema. The extraction is imperfect. The data is available now, not in six months.

Then master iteratively. Build disambiguation pipelines that resolve the fact that "Herceptin," "trastuzumab," and "anti-HER2 monoclonal antibody" all refer to the same drug. Each iteration improves quality. Critically, the data is usable at every stage. The pattern: ingest natively, store as-is, master iteratively, use continuously.

The Hazards of External Data

External data is not without its hazards. In pharmaceutical R&D, external academic datasets sometimes contain inconsistent compound identifiers, outdated gene nomenclature, or conflicting clinical endpoints that can confound analysis if taken at face value. One particularly common challenge involves integrating data from ClinicalTrials.gov, where protocol amendments create versioning complexity. The same trial can appear in multiple states, and if the versioning is not carefully managed, the analysis can be misleading. The lesson is not to avoid external data but to invest in the curation and quality processes required to make it trustworthy. Just as a racing team would never load weather data into their strategy models without validating its accuracy and timeliness, organizations must build robust quality controls around external data ingestion.

+tellic, one of the racing program's sponsors and a platform I have seen deployed in enterprise settings, has spent more than a decade on this problem. Their platform ingests research publications, grants, preprints, clinical trials, patents, and proprietary data, then uses biomedical natural language processing to link entities into preferred ontologies, resolving the naming disparities that make cross-source analysis so treacherous. The result is a unified biomedical knowledge graph that allows pharmaceutical companies to search and analyze across fifty years of research data as a single, coherent asset. It illustrates what becomes possible when an organization invests in the hard work of curation at scale.

The financial services industry offers another compelling example. Banks and investment firms are increasingly building proprietary intelligence from external data sources rather than relying on the same market feed available to every competitor. Some use satellite imagery of retail parking lots to estimate quarterly earnings before they are reported. Others analyze shipping container movements to predict supply chain disruptions. Credit risk teams are incorporating alternative data, from utility payment patterns to mobile device metadata, to assess borrowers who lack traditional credit histories. Each of these is the financial equivalent of building your own weather model: using external data that others have not thought to integrate, creating an informational advantage that compounds over time.

The cost of ignoring external data can be severe. I have seen organizations learn this the hard way. One pharmaceutical company I advised had built an impressive internal analytics capability but treated external data as an afterthought. When a competitor published real-world evidence from electronic health records showing that their drug performed better in a specific patient subpopulation, it caught the company flat-footed. The competitor used that evidence to secure a favorable guideline update, shifting prescribing patterns across the market in a matter of months. The data had been available to both companies. Only one had invested in the infrastructure to find it, analyze it, and act on it. By the time the other company responded, the market share shift had already occurred. In racing terms, they were watching their own telemetry while the competitor was building weather models.

The Competitive Imperative

The racing teams that invest in weather prediction models do not do it because it is interesting. They do it because it wins races. The data that matters most might not be the data you generate yourself. It might be the data that is already out there, beyond the track walls, waiting for someone to integrate it into their decision-making process.

Go get it.

Key Lesson: The track is always changing. The best teams watch the horizon and adapt before the competition does.

Business Translation: External data, emerging technologies, and new ways of thinking can unlock advantages you can't find looking inward.

Racer Tip: Study your competitors, but don't copy them. Innovate your own line.

Monday Action: Identify one external data source or trend you are not using today that could create value.

CHAPTER 8

The Hidden Telemetry

Principle 4: Find Unique Data Sources That Your Competitors Have Not Discovered

External data becomes a commodity the moment everyone has access to it. The competitive advantage lives in data sources that your competitors have not discovered yet – sources that may exist in entirely different industries, hiding in workflows that have nothing to do with your business.

When I was the Chief Data Officer for Samsung Mobile, I spent a great deal of time thinking about a problem that seemed like it should have been easy to solve: understanding how people were using their phones and, more importantly, when they were switching from one device to another. If you are a mobile phone manufacturer in a brutally competitive market, knowing that a customer just traded in a Galaxy for an iPhone (or vice versa) is among the most valuable signals in the world. It tells you whether your marketing is working, whether your latest hardware refresh is convincing, and which demographic segments are drifting away from your ecosystem.

The trouble is that this data is surprisingly hard to come by. Carriers have some of it, but their incentives for sharing are misaligned with yours. Social media sentiment gives you a vague directional read. Retail sell-through data arrives weeks late and is riddled with gaps. None of these sources offered the granularity or the timeliness that I needed.

So, I struck a relationship with a bank, a national bank, one of the top four in the United States. A friend of mine had recently become the head of data for the bank, which gave me a way in the door. The conversation that followed would have been strong regardless of the personal connection.

If that partnership seems unlikely, good. It should seem unlikely. Why on earth would a bank have useful data for a mobile phone manufacturer? The answer is hiding in plain sight, in the palm of your hand.

Think about what happens the moment you buy a new phone. You bring it home, you start transferring your apps, and one of the very first things you set up is your banking application. Banks are required to verify your identity before letting you access your account, and part of that verification process captures what device you are using. The bank knows your phone model. The bank knows when you switched. Because people set up their banking app almost immediately, the bank knows it in something close to real time.

It gets better. The bank also knows what device you were using before. So, it has an exact record of switching behavior: from which manufacturer to which manufacturer, on what date, in what geography. When you aggregate that data across millions of banking customers, you end up with a picture of the mobile device market that is, frankly, better than anything the carriers themselves possess.

Now, here is the critical part: the data was aggregated: just the device type, switching data, and a small number of demographic items. No individual-level PII. I did not need to know who these people were. I did not need names, account numbers, or any personally identifiable information. What I needed was aggregate switching behavior by zip code and device type. With just this small amount of data, we could see patterns like: a man between the ages of twenty and twenty-nine living in the Los Angeles area switched from an Apple iPhone to a Samsung Galaxy in May after using the iPhone for two years. This level of granularity, without ever identifying a single individual, was enormously valuable for understanding competitive dynamics in the mobile device market. How many people in the Dallas-Fort Worth metro area switched from an iPhone 13 to a Galaxy S22 last month? How many went the other direction? The bank could provide that data without violating a single privacy regulation, because what I was asking for was demographic pattern data, not individual consumer records.

For the bank, this was a trivial extraction, a byproduct of processes they were already running for fraud detection and device authentication. For Samsung, it was a goldmine. It provided a completely unique data source that was extremely actionable, and one that no other mobile manufacturer had thought to pursue.

That partnership changed the way I think about data sourcing forever. The lesson was not about banking or telecommunications. It was about the power of cross-industry thinking: the data you need may already exist in an industry that has no idea it is valuable to you.

Boardroom Translation

Everyone in your industry buys the same syndicated data, runs the same surveys, licenses the same third-party feeds. The dashboards converge and the insights have the shelf life of yesterday's bread. In business terms: the data equivalent of building your own weather model is finding a data source in an adjacent industry that your competitors have not thought to look for. The advantage is not in having more data. It is in having different data.

The Racing Parallel

When we built the Big Data in Action racing team, we operated in a world where every competitor had access to the same on-car telemetry. Speed, throttle position, brake pressure, lateral G-forces, engine temperature. The sensor packages were standardized, and the analysis tools were commercially available to anyone willing to pay for them. If you wanted a competitive edge from data, you could not get it simply by measuring the same things everyone else was measuring and hoping to analyze them a little bit faster.

So, we started looking at all kinds of different data sources, trying to figure out whether we could use something in a unique way that would give us a little bit of a competitive advantage. The weather models I described in Chapter 7 were one example, but the principle went further. We acquired the kind of granular, location-specific weather modeling data that agricultural companies and energy traders use, data that was freely available but that nobody else in our competitive class had thought to layer into race strategy models. Temperature, humidity, and wind direction affected tire grip, engine performance, and braking distances in ways that our competitors were not modeling. Cost of acquisition: close to zero. Competitive value: significant.

That experience reinforced what the Samsung-bank partnership had taught me: the most powerful data sources are often the ones hiding in someone else's workflow.

The Retailer Who Became a Weatherman

Another example illustrates this principle from a different angle. During my time leading IBM's Business Analytics and Optimization practice in growth markets, I worked with a major retail chain that was struggling with inventory allocation across hundreds of stores. They were using the same demand forecasting tools as every other retailer, built on the same historical sales data and seasonal patterns. The forecasts were decent but undifferentiated. Every competitor was converging on similar predictions because the underlying methodology and data were identical.

We asked a simple question: What data exists outside the retail industry that could improve store-level demand prediction? The answer turned out to be hyperlocal weather data combined with municipal event calendars.

Every city publishes a calendar of permitted events: parades, festivals, road closures, sporting events, concerts. That data is freely available in municipal records. When you overlay it with store locations, you can predict which stores will see foot traffic surges or declines on specific days. A street festival three blocks from a downtown store should drive up walk-in traffic. A major highway closure near a suburban location will suppress it. None of this was captured in the retailer's point-of-sale history, but it was entirely predictable from public data sources.

The weather component went deeper than simply predicting rain. We found that the rate of temperature change mattered more than the absolute temperature. A sudden ten-degree drop in temperature in September drove a spike in jacket and cold-weather accessory purchases that a gradual decline over two weeks did not, even if both periods reached the same low temperature. The surprise of the weather shift triggered purchasing behavior, not the weather itself. That insight came from correlating granular weather data (the kind that energy companies use to predict heating demand) with transaction-level sales data at specific store locations.

Neither of these data sources was secret, proprietary, or expensive. They were invisible to an industry that had been looking at its own sales data for so long that it had forgotten to look out the window.

When the Data Comes to You

Not every unique data source requires you to go looking for it. Sometimes the most valuable data is already being generated within your own organization, by processes that nobody has thought to instrument.

At one company I worked with, the customer service call center was recording every call for quality assurance purposes. Those recordings sat on servers, accumulating by the terabyte, listened to only when a specific complaint needed to be reviewed. No one had thought to analyze them at scale. When we applied natural language processing to those recordings, we discovered patterns that the structured data from the CRM system completely missed. Customers were mentioning competitor products by name and describing features they wished existed. They were expressing frustrations that never made it into the formal complaint categories because the call center agents did not have a checkbox for "customer is considering switching to a competitor."

The data was not external. It was not purchased. It was not even new. It had been accumulating for years. It was unique in the sense that no one, including the company itself, had recognized its analytical value. The most hidden telemetry sometimes turns out to be the telemetry you have been generating all along but never thought to use.

The Art of Cross-Industry Data Thinking

The breakthrough comes from looking sideways.

Hedge funds have pioneered one of the most striking examples. They purchase satellite imagery of retail parking lots and use computer vision to count cars at specific times. The fullness of a Walmart parking lot at two o'clock on a Saturday correlates surprisingly well with quarterly same-store sales figures. The parking lot has always been there. The satellites have been overhead for years. What changed is that someone thought to connect the two – to see telemetry where others saw only asphalt. That insight was worth billions. It came not from a better financial model, but from a better data source imported from an entirely different domain.

Or consider how shipping container tracking data, originally collected for logistics, became one of the most powerful leading indicators of global economic activity. The data existed. It was sitting in a different industry's filing cabinet.

The data that will give you a competitive advantage already exists. It is being collected by someone who does not realize its value to you.

A Framework for Finding Hidden Telemetry

After three decades of data leadership across telecommunications, pharmaceuticals, consumer electronics, and several other industries, I have developed a systematic approach to identifying unique data sources. It is not magic. It is a disciplined process of asking the right questions.

Step One: Map the Decision, Not the Data. Start with the decision you are trying to improve and work backward. Do not begin by inventorying what data you have. That approach anchors you to the familiar. Instead, ask: *What would I need to know, in an ideal world, to make this decision perfectly?* Write down every variable and every signal, no matter how impractical it seems. This creates your wish list.

Step Two: Identify the Natural Collectors. For each item on your wish list, ask: *Who, during their normal business operations, would naturally observe or capture this information?* The answer is almost never limited to companies in your own industry. Banks observe purchasing behavior. Insurance companies observe risk events. Utility companies observe occupancy patterns. Transportation companies observe economic activity. Social media platforms observe sentiment shifts. The question is not *Who sells this data?* but *Who generates this data as a byproduct of something else they are doing?*

Step Three: Assess the Privacy and Ethics Landscape. Before pursuing any external data source, you must rigorously evaluate the privacy implications. The Samsung-bank example worked exactly because the data was aggregated and anonymized. I did not care who was switching phones. I cared about how many people in a given geography were switching, and in which direction. This distinction is not just legally important. It is ethically essential. Any data partnership that requires you to compromise individual privacy is not worth the competitive advantage, full stop. There are almost always ways to structure the exchange so that you get the aggregate patterns you need without touching personally identifiable information.

Step Four: Evaluate the Competitive Exclusivity. A data source is only *unique* if your competitors are not already using it. Part of your assessment should include understanding how widely available this data is and how quickly it could become commoditized. The parking-lot satellite imagery example is instructive: the first funds to use it made enormous returns, but within a few years, the technique was widely known and the advantage eroded. Ideally, you want data sources where the relationship itself, not just the data, creates the moat. The Samsung-bank partnership was valuable partly because the relationship was exclusive. The bank had no incentive to offer the same data to every phone manufacturer.

Step Five: Build the Integration Path. Finding a unique data source is only half the battle. You also need to integrate it into your decision-making workflows in a way that is repeatable and trusted. A one-time analysis is interesting. A continuous feed that updates your models in real time is transformative. Invest in the engineering required to make the data operational, not just analytical.

Open Data and the Scouting Mindset

Governments sit on treasure troves of freely available data that the private sector universally ignores: census data, weather records, transportation data, building permits, court filings. Companies ignore it because it lacks packaging – inconvenient formats, inconsistent schemas, poor documentation. That effort to clean and integrate is the moat. In our racing program, we used publicly available historical race results that anyone could download. The data was free; the effort to clean and normalize it was our competitive advantage.

No industry has embraced unique data sourcing more aggressively than finance. Hedge funds routinely purchase credit card transaction data, mobile phone location data, job posting data, and app download statistics. The lesson is not to copy their specific sources but their mindset: they have institutionalized asking "What data exists that could give us a two-day edge?" Every industry should have this function. It does not require a massive budget – just the creativity to look and the engineering effort to operationalize.

The Data Partnership Playbook

The Samsung-bank partnership succeeded because we led with mutual value, not data extraction. Samsung offered mobile device insights valuable to the bank's digital strategy; the bank offered aggregate switching data valuable to us. Neither side felt exploited.

Data partnerships work best when data never leaves the originating infrastructure – you transfer aggregated insights or run analyses in a secure environment the data owner controls. Start with a single use case, demonstrate value within ninety days, and expand from there.

The Perishable Advantage

Unique data sources do not stay unique forever. Competitors will discover them, vendors will commercialize them. This is why finding unique sources must be ongoing – a capability, not a project. I call this the **data scouting cycle**: discover, evaluate, operationalize, and sunset. The hidden telemetry is out there. Your job is to build an organization that never stops looking.

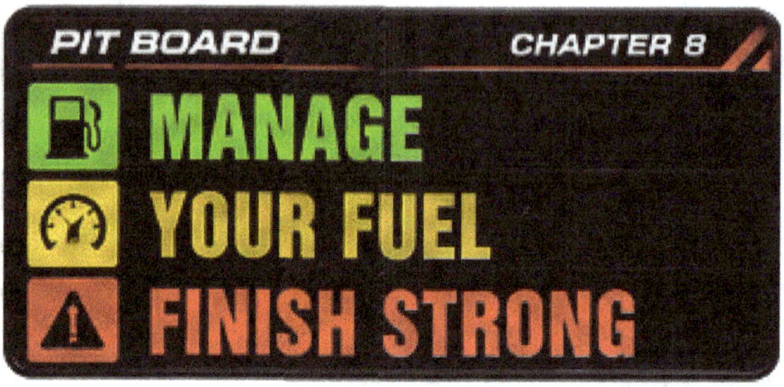

Key Lesson: Resources are finite. The best teams manage their fuel - time, budget, talent, and data - through the entire race, not just the first lap.

Business Translation: Data programs burn out when they start too fast or chase too many priorities. Sustainable pacing wins.

Racer Tip: Lift and coast when you need to. Smart conservation wins races.

Monday Action: Review your top data initiatives. Stop, slow, or sequence one that is draining more fuel than it returns.

CHAPTER 9

Racing Through the Archives

Principle 5: Find New Ways to Compare Using Historical Data

I remember presenting a concept to a pharmaceutical leadership team and watching the reaction move across the room like a wave. The head of clinical operations leaned forward and said, "We have never measured that." He paused. "But we absolutely should, because I can tell you right now that at least half of those delays are caused by our own internal governance process."

What we had shown him was simple: the gaps between his company's clinical trial phases, the unmeasured white space between the end of Phase I and the start of Phase II, were consistently longer than their competitors'. Not by a little. By months. The data to make this comparison has been publicly available for years. Nobody had thought about looking at it.

That moment captures the essence of this chapter's principle: the richest insights in historical data are often hiding not in what everyone measures, but in what nobody measures: the gaps, the transitions, the negative space between the events that fill the dashboards and the quarterly reviews. I will walk through the full white space story later in this chapter. First, I want to show you where the principle came from: the racetrack.

Building the Archive

Every racing circuit has a memory. The asphalt remembers the rubber laid down by a thousand previous races. The walls remember the impact. The record books remember everything. The same drivers driving the same cars go back to the same tracks year after year. That fact, which might seem like a mundane observation about the structure of a racing calendar, is a profound analytical opportunity. It means that historical data is not just background context. It is a predictive resource.

We downloaded all previous IMSA race results from results.imsa.com – a remarkable open archive of drivers, lap times, pit stops, positions, and incidents. From this data, we built a profile for every driver we were likely to compete against: how aggressive in opening laps, how long their typical stint, their accident history, whether they overdrive in rain or become conservative, how their performance degrades with fatigue.

This was not revolutionary computer science. It was disciplined historical analysis applied with a specific purpose: converting the past into competitive advantage. When we arrived at the circuit, we had a playbook. We knew which teams historically favored early pit strategies (so we could stay out longer), which driver-car combinations showed strong qualifying but fading race pace (so we wouldn't burn tires chasing them), and which drivers had high contact rates at specific corner types (so we could adjust positioning).

None of these guaranteed outcomes. It shifted probabilities in our favor, and in a sport where the margin between podium and mid-pack is razor-thin, shifted probabilities are everything.

One of the most instructive examples came from the NASA six-hour endurance race at Utah Motorsports Campus. The team that won the race did not have the fastest lap times. Not even close. They had qualified in the top five, demonstrating they had the raw pace, but during the race, they were running several seconds per lap slower than the leaders.

Their strategy was smart and data driven. By extending their time on track, running at a slightly reduced pace that dramatically extended their fuel window, they were able to eliminate at least one pit stop that every other team had to make. A pit stop in endurance racing can consume four to eight minutes, depending on whether you are adding fuel, changing tires, or swapping drivers. By running a few seconds slower per lap but staying on track while others were burning time in the pits, they effectively gained more time than they lost. A slightly slower lap time, sustained over a longer stint, was worth more than raw speed punctuated by expensive pit stops.

This is the kind of insight that only emerges from historical analysis. By studying how teams approached fuel strategy across previous races at the same circuit, we could have predicted (and in future races, did predict) which competitors would employ a conservation strategy versus an all-out pace strategy. The data was there in the archives. It simply required looking at it through the right lens.

Beyond Simple Benchmarking

Most organizations do use historical data. The problem is how they use it. The default approach is simple time-series comparison: How did we do this quarter compared to last? How do our cycle times compare to the industry average? These comparisons tell you whether things got better or worse, but they rarely tell you why.

The White Space: Finding What Nobody Measures

During my time in pharmaceutical data and analytics, I spent a great deal of time studying clinical trials. There is a vast amount of publicly available data about clinical trials because every trial conducted anywhere in the world gets registered and eventually published. You can see what drugs were tested, what indications they targeted, how many patients were enrolled, how long the trials lasted, and what the outcomes were.

Most organizations that analyze this data do the obvious thing: they compare their own trial performance to the competition. How long did it take them to complete a Phase II trial? How long does it take us? How many patients did they enroll per site? How many do we enroll? These are reasonable questions, and the benchmarking they enable is useful. It is not where the real insight lives, though.

Real insight lives in the white space.

When I say, *white space*, I mean the gaps between the structured milestones, the time periods that nobody thinks to measure because they fall outside the formal boundaries of the process being studied. In clinical trials, the most interesting white space is not the trial itself. It is the gap between trials.

Consider this: a pharmaceutical company completes a successful Phase I trial. The drug shows safety and preliminary efficacy. The team celebrates. Then… nothing happens for eight months before the Phase II trial begins.

Why?

That eight-month gap is not captured in any clinical trial database. The trial registries record when each phase started and ended, but they do not record what happened in between. Yet that gap, that white space, is where some of the most important and actionable insights hide.

That gap may not be a scientific problem. It is a business problem. The delay between Phase I and Phase II might be caused by regulatory paperwork that took longer than expected. It might be a budget approval process that required three rounds of committee review. A manufacturing scale-up challenge. A strategic reprioritization at the portfolio level that bumped this program down the queue. Or the simple, maddening reality that the clinical operations team was already committed to launching two other trials and did not have the bandwidth to start a third.

None of these causes are visible in the traditional clinical trial metrics. Every single one of them is actionable. If you can identify that your white space between phases is consistently longer than your competitors' white space, you have found a source of competitive disadvantage that has nothing to do with science and everything to do with operational efficiency. Operational efficiency can be fixed.

Boardroom Translation

A racing team does not just measure cornering speed — they measure the gap between the corner exit and the moment the driver gets back on the throttle. In business terms: stop measuring only your formal process milestones. Measure the gaps between them. The white space between your Phase I completion and your Phase II initiation, between your product decision and your launch execution, between your strategy approval and your first hire, is where the most actionable inefficiencies hide. The data is usually already there. Nobody has thought to look at it.

The power of this insight is that it reframes what you are looking at. Instead of comparing trial performance (which is heavily influenced by the biology of the drug and the design of the study, factors that are difficult to change) you are comparing business process efficiency, which is entirely within your control.

The data to make this comparison is right there, in the public record, available to anyone who thinks to look for it. The clinical trial registries publish start and end dates for every phase. The white space is computable from publicly available timestamps. No special data access nor expensive data vendor is required. Just a unique way of looking at information that has been sitting in plain view all along. That is why the head of clinical operations I described at the opening of this chapter reacted the way he did. He immediately knew what to do about it, because the insight pointed to something entirely within his control.

A top ten pharmaceutical company engaged Ramsey International to examine the duration of their clinical trials for new drug candidates. The question seemed straightforward: why do our trials take so long compared to competitors?

When we decomposed the timeline, the answer was not in the phases themselves. The actual conduct of Phase I, Phase II, and Phase III trials was competitive. The problem was hiding in the white space between phases. The gap between completing Phase I and initiating Phase II ranged from three months to eighteen months across different programs. Best-in-class competitors were consistently transitioning in as little as three months. Some of this company's programs took six times as long to make the handoff.

The root cause analysis told us something we did not expect. In several cases, the delay was driven by a deceptively simple operational constraint: the company did not have sufficient manufactured product to conduct the next phase of trials. Drug manufacturing is expensive and time-consuming, and the traditional approach was to wait for Phase I results before committing to the manufacturing investment for Phase II quantities. It was a perfectly rational, risk-averse strategy, and it was costing them months of competitive advantage on every program.

The solution required a calculated risk that mirrors a racing decision perfectly. Just as a driver must commit to carrying more speed into a corner before knowing with certainty that the car will hold, trusting the data, the preparation, and the physics, the pharmaceutical company had to begin manufacturing the drug compound before Phase I results were finalized. Start building the product on the bet that Phase I would succeed. If it failed, the manufacturing investment would be lost. If it succeeded, the Phase I-to-Phase II gap collapsed from months to weeks.

The risk paid high returns. This "at-risk manufacturing" approach, informed by historical success rates and competitive benchmarking from the white space analysis, allowed the company to compress their phase transitions and bring therapies to patients faster.

The Gap Analysis Concept

The clinical trial white space is an example of a broader analytical technique that I call *gap analysis*, and it applies far beyond pharmaceuticals.

Every business process has a formal workflow, the documented steps that are measured, managed, and optimized. Most business processes have informal gaps: transitions, handoffs, waiting periods, and decision delays that fall between the formal steps. These gaps are almost never instrumented and are rarely tracked, yet they frequently account for a larger share of total cycle time than the formal steps themselves.

In manufacturing, the gap between "order received" and "production scheduled" is often longer and more variable than the production process itself. I worked with a manufacturer that measured every step of its production process with Six Sigma rigor but had never measured the scheduling gap. When they did, they found that forty percent of their total order-to-delivery time was consumed by internal scheduling negotiations between plants, none of which was tracked in any system. The production floor was optimized. The white space between the order and the production floor was chaos.

In software development, the gap between "code complete" and "deployed to production" can stretch for weeks in organizations with cumbersome release processes. In sales, the gap between "proposal delivered" and "decision received" is one of the most consequential time periods in the entire revenue cycle, and it is almost entirely invisible to the CRM system.

Historical data makes gap analysis possible because you need enough observations to distinguish between a gap that is structurally inherent in your process and a gap that is anomalous and therefore fixable. A single instance of an eight-month delay between Phase I and Phase II tells you nothing. It was a one-time event caused by unusual circumstances. Twenty instances of delays ranging from three to fourteen months, clustered by therapeutic area, geography, and organizational unit, start to reveal patterns that point directly to root causes.

The historical archive is the laboratory where these patterns become visible. Without it, every gap looks like an exception. With it, the exceptions reveal the rules.

Predictive Profiles from Historical Data

When we built driver profiles for our racing competitors, we were doing something more sophisticated than simple benchmarking. We were building predictive behavioral models from historical patterns. This technique, creating multi-dimensional profiles of entities based on their historical behavior and then using those profiles to predict future actions, is one of the most underutilized applications of historical data in business.

Consider how this applies to competitive intelligence. Most companies track their competitors' moves as they happen: product launches, pricing changes, executive hires. This is reactive intelligence. You learn about the move after it has been made. If you build a historical profile of a competitor's behavior, examining how they have responded to market shifts in the past, how long they typically take to follow a competitor's pricing move, whether they tend to invest in R&D during downturns or pull back, you can start to predict their next move before they make it.

In my early career at IBM, I worked on what would now be called predictive analytics for churn in the mobile phone industry. My dissertation research was on the impact of inferred social networks on churn prediction models, the idea that you could predict whether someone would leave their mobile carrier not just by looking at their own usage patterns, but by looking at whether their friends and family members had recently churned. That work led to a US patent and taught me an enduring lesson: historical behavior patterns, when combined with relational context, become predictive in ways that neither dimension achieves alone.

The same principle applied to our racing driver profiles. A driver's historical lap times at a specific circuit, considered in isolation, gave us a rough performance baseline. When we combined that with their stint length patterns, their behavior in traffic, and their historical reliability record, the profile became really predictive. We could anticipate not just how fast they would be, but how they would race. That shaped our strategy in ways that raw speed data never could.

The F1 Historical Data Archive

To appreciate the scale of what is possible with historical racing data, consider Formula 1. As we explored in Chapter 3, F1's partnership with AWS has digitized over seventy years of race data, every qualifying session, every race result, every pit stop, every fastest lap.

The real power of that archive is not in the broadcast graphics. It is in the patterns that emerge when you look at seventy years of data through an analytical lens. How has the importance of qualifying position changed over time as circuits have evolved? How does the historical relationship between tire strategy and race outcome vary by circuit type, whether street circuits, permanent facilities, or high-speed ovals? When a team introduces a major car upgrade, how does the historical data suggest the competitive order will shift?

F1 teams with the resources to mine this archive have built models that go far beyond lap time prediction. They model strategic scenarios using decades of data about how races at specific circuits have historically unfolded: where safety cars tend to appear, how weather typically evolves over the course of a race weekend, what pit stop windows have historically proven optimal. The past, rigorously analyzed, becomes a rehearsal for the future.

The scale difference is instructive: a full season of IMSA GT4 racing generates twenty percent of the data volume of a single Formula 1 team's weekend. The analytical principles are identical regardless of budget: comparing driver profiles across historical data, identifying patterns in competitor strategy, finding the white space in performance gaps.

Finding the Negative Space

The white space concept is part of a larger philosophy: analyzing the negative space – what did not happen, what was not recorded, what falls between the measurements.

Consider customer churn. Most models focus on the customers who left. The negative space – the customers who should have left but did not – is equally valuable. What kept them? The non-events are invisible unless you deliberately go looking for them.

Or consider fraud detection. Traditional approaches model what fraud looks like. The negative space approach asks: What normal activity is conspicuously absent? A credit card that suddenly stops being used at a customer's regular grocery store might signal compromise, even without any overtly fraudulent transactions. The absence of expected behavior is itself a signal.

Historical data makes negative space analysis possible because you need a baseline of "normal" to detect the absence of normal. That baseline can only be established through sustained observation over time.

Creative Approaches to Historical Analysis

Beyond gap analysis and negative space, there are several other techniques for extracting non-obvious value from historical data that I have seen work across multiple industries.

Cohort Comparison Across Eras. Instead of comparing this year to last year, compare cohorts of similar entities across different time periods. How did the class of drugs approved in 2015 perform in their first five years on the market compared to the class approved in 2010? The answer reveals not just performance trends but shifts in the regulatory environment and changes in market access, all of which are invisible in a simple year-over-year comparison.

Analogical Reasoning from Adjacent Domains. When your own historical data is insufficient, borrow someone else's. A startup launching a new category of consumer products has no historical sales data for that product. It can, however, study the launch trajectories of analogous products from other categories: the adoption curve of streaming services, the diffusion pattern of electric vehicles, the growth trajectory of meal kit delivery companies. Historical data from adjacent domains, mapped through analogy, can serve as a surprisingly effective substitute for domain-specific history.

Regime Detection. Most historical analysis implicitly assumes that the world operates under consistent rules. Markets and industries go through regime changes, periods where the fundamental dynamics shift. A historical model trained in data from a stable regime will fail spectacularly when the regime changes. Smart historical analysis explicitly looks for these breakpoints: When did the rules change? What triggered the shift? What does the post-shift regime look like compared to the pre-shift regime? In racing, a major regulation change (a new tire specification, a new fuel restriction, a revised aerodynamic package) creates a regime change that makes pre-change historical data less predictive. The teams that recognize this fastest and recalibrate their models gain a significant advantage.

Trajectory Analysis. Instead of comparing static snapshots, compare trajectories. Where an entity is at any single point in time is less interesting than the direction and velocity of its movement over time. A competitor whose market share is 15% and falling tells a quite different story than a competitor whose market share is 15% and rising, even though the snapshot looks identical. Historical data enables trajectory analysis, which in turn enables prediction. Trajectories, once established, tend to persist unless acted upon by an external force.

The Telecommunications Lesson

This example brings several of these historical analysis techniques together, drawn from my work in the telecommunications industry.

When I was working on churn prediction at IBM, we had access to years of historical customer data from mobile carriers. The standard approach was to build a model using recent data, the last twelve months of customer behavior, to predict who would churn in the next thirty days. Industry-standard methodology, industry-standard results: moderate accuracy and moderate business value.

We tried something different. We went back further, much further, into the historical archive and built what we called "lifecycle models." Instead of treating every customer as if they were in the same analytical frame, we segmented them by how long they had been customers and modeled the churn dynamics of each lifecycle stage separately. A customer who had been with the carrier for six months exhibited vastly different churn patterns than a customer who had been there for six years. The six-month customer was still in the evaluation phase. They were comparing the carrier to their previous provider, and their churn triggers were related to network quality and pricing surprises. The six-year customer had long since stopped comparing. Their churn triggers were life events: moving to a new city, children leaving home, downsizing in retirement.

The historical data made this possible because we needed enough longitudinal depth to observe full customer lifecycles. A twelve-month training window could not distinguish between a two-year customer who was about to churn and a two-year customer who would stay for another decade, because both looked the same in the recent data. Five years of historical data revealed the trajectories, the subtle behavioral shifts that preceded churn at each lifecycle stage, and our models improved dramatically as a result.

This is the kind of insight that only the archives can provide. You cannot shortcut it with better algorithms or faster processing. You need the depth of time.

The Organizational Challenge of Historical Data

In most organizations, historical data is a mess. Systems have been migrated, schemas have changed, data has been lost to decommissioned platforms. This is a real obstacle but not a reason to abandon historical analysis – it is a reason to invest in data archaeology.

Our racing data was far from perfect: inconsistent driver names, changing car numbers, different classification schemes across series. The key lesson was to look not at raw data but at the direction of the data. Trends and relative performance patterns remain surprisingly stable even when conditions shift.

If you are a data leader, ask your team: How far back can we run a consistent analysis? If less than five years, you have a data archaeology problem worth solving.

The Compounding Nature of Historical Insight

There is one final dimension to historical data analysis that I want to highlight: Historical analysis compounds.

When you build a driver profile in Year One, it gives you a moderate advantage. In Year Two, you add another season's worth of data, and the profile becomes more robust and more predictive. By Year Five, your profiles incorporate patterns that span multiple car generations and regulation changes, across multiple career phases for each driver. The analytical asset appreciates over time, like a fine wine or a well-managed investment portfolio.

The same compounding dynamic applies in business. A pharmaceutical company that has been systematically measuring white space between clinical trial phases for five years has a richer, more granular understanding of its own operational dynamics than a company that just started measuring last quarter. A retailer with ten years of integrated demand data, correlated with weather, events, and competitive activity, can predict next month's sales with an accuracy that a newcomer to that analysis simply cannot match.

This is the true strategic argument for investing in historical data: the advantage compounds, and it is impossible for a competitor to replicate quickly. A competitor can copy your algorithm. A competitor can license the same data vendors. A competitor cannot conjure ten years of clean, integrated, consistently measured historical data out of thin air. That takes time, and time is the one resource that cannot be purchased.

The Lesson from the Archives

The archives are not a museum. They are a laboratory. The past is not behind you. It is underneath you, the foundation on which every future insight is built. Race through the archives with purpose, and you will find the signals that everyone else overlooked because they were too busy staring at the present.

Bringing It All Together: The Five Racing Principles

Over the preceding chapters, we have explored each of the five racing principles in depth, from their origins on the track to their application in the boardroom. The following illustration brings them together in a single view, mapping each principle from its racing context to its business application. Think of it as your pit board for the rest of this book and beyond: a reference you can return to as you apply these ideas in your own organization.

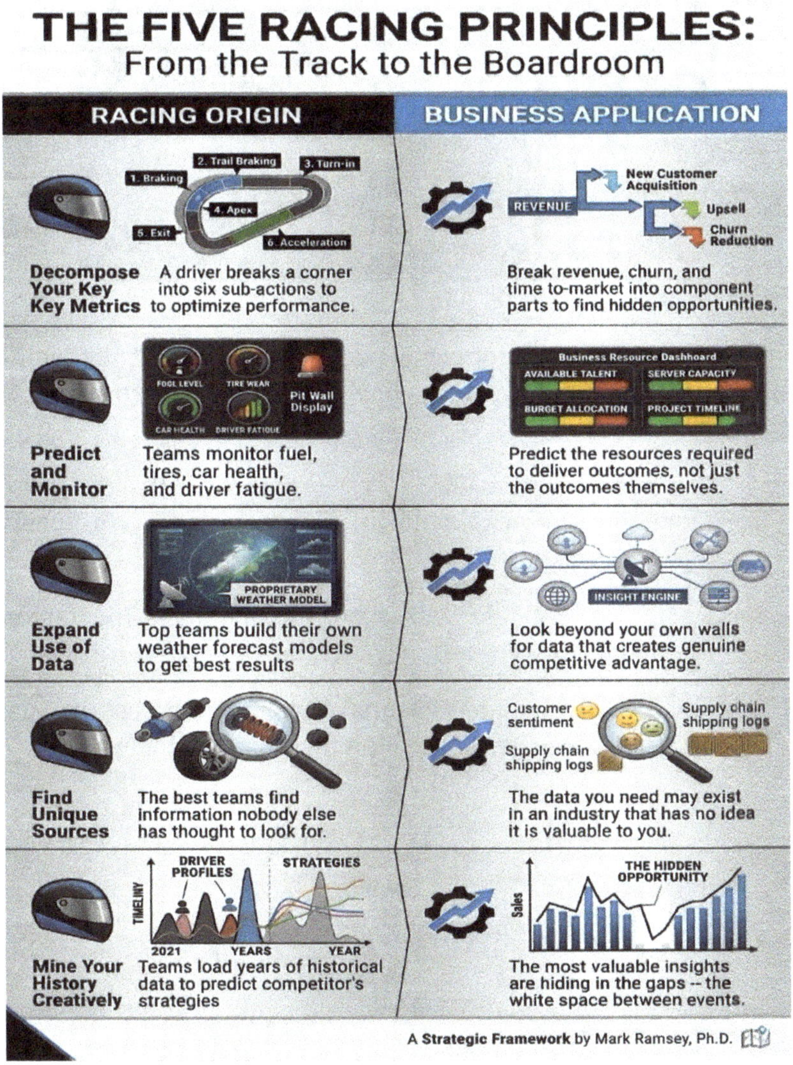

Figure 9.1: The Five Racing Principles, showing how each principle maps from its racing origin to its business application.

Key Lesson: History won't repeat exactly, but it rhymes. Your data archive is a strategic asset for learning and prediction.

Business Translation: An organized, trusted data foundation unlocks pattern discovery, better forecasts, and faster experimentation.

Racer Tip: Validate with data, not memory. The fastest teams turn history into advantage.

Monday Action: Identify one historical dataset you can analyze to answer a question that matters today.

Part III

Lessons from the Cockpit:

Leadership, Culture, and Resilience

CHAPTER 10

When the Car Goes Airborne

Managing Failure, Risk, and Resilience

Strapping on the helmet before a stint at Watkins Glen. In both racing and data leadership, the preparation before the critical moment defines the outcome.

In Chapter 1, I described two photographs on my desk: the podium celebration and the crumpled race car. The thrill of victory and the agony of defeat. At my MIT presentation, it was the second photograph that went up first, before I talked about data ecosystems, before I walked through lap telemetry or described our analytics architecture. ABC's *Wide World of Sports* used to call it "the agony of defeat," that famous footage of the ski jumper tumbling end over end. Every racer knows that image has a motorsport equivalent. Sometimes you are standing on the podium, spraying champagne. Sometimes a car lands on top of yours at over a hundred miles per hour, and you are done for the day.

This chapter is about the second kind of day. More importantly, it is about what happens next, and what those worst-case moments in racing can teach every data leader about managing failure and building the kind of resilience that enables you to come back and compete again.

The Corkscrew

WeatherTech Raceway Laguna Seca sits along the central California coast near Monterey, carved into the golden hills above the Pacific. It is one of the most famous circuits in North America, and if you know anything about it, you know about the Corkscrew. The Corkscrew is a sequence of turns near the top of the track where the road drops roughly eight stories through a blind left-right combination. You cannot see the second apex when you enter the first. You are braking hard, turning in, and falling, quite literally falling, through a compression that pushes the car down into its suspension as gravity and lateral force combine in a way that makes your stomach float for just a moment. It is exhilarating. It is also the kind of corner where small mistakes become large ones very quickly, because at those speeds and with that elevation change, the car is right on the edge of its mechanical grip.

I loved racing at Laguna Seca. The track has eleven turns, each with its own personality, and the elevation changes reward precision. What happened to me there during the IMSA Michelin Pilot Challenge in October 2019, an endurance race in our Mercedes-AMG GT4, had nothing to do with the Corkscrew itself. It had to do with strategy, tire degradation, and a chain of events that no amount of data could have fully prevented.

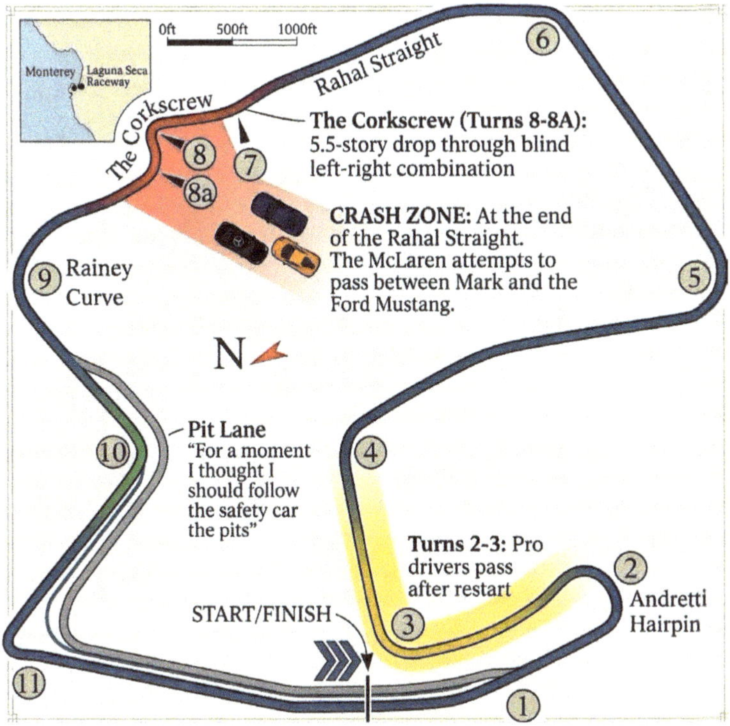

Figure 10.1: Laguna Seca Track Map, showing the circuit layout with key locations from the crash narrative, including the Corkscrew, the restart zone at Turn 11, and the crash zone approximately 100 yards before the Corkscrew.

The Setup

You read the strategy in Chapter 2: the yellow flag, the cars ahead pitting, our engineer's calculation that staying out could turn a one-stop strategy into a winning position. The math worked. The strategy was sound.

What I did not convey in Chapter 2 was how it felt. The yellow had bunched the entire field nose-to-tail. When the green flag dropped, thirty-five cars would accelerate simultaneously, most of them driven by professionals on fresh tires and full tanks.

I was scared. I was an amateur driver on destroyed tires, and the thirty-four cars behind me were mostly driven by professionals on fresh rubber.

The Moment

The restart came. Green flag. I got on the throttle and tried to hold my line, knowing exactly what was about to happen. The cars behind me had vastly more grip, and they were going to start coming through. My job was simple in concept and terrifying in execution: stay out of their way while losing as little time as possible. Do not wreck the car.

A number of the pro drivers passed me at Turn 2 and Turn 3. That was expected. As we passed Turn 6 and headed up toward the famous Corkscrew, I found myself running side by side with a pink Ford Mustang. I was on the right side and he was on the left. About a hundred yards from the Corkscrew, a McLaren driver thought he could push his car between the two of us to get in front. There was not enough space.

The sloped front of the McLaren hit the Ford Mustang in the right rear. When a car traveling at over a hundred miles per hour makes contact with the rear quarter of another car at just the wrong angle, physics takes over in a spectacular and terrifying way. The Ford Mustang launched into the air. Not a small hop. It went fully, completely airborne, flew over my hood, and came crashing down the front of my car.

The speed at impact was approximately a hundred and ten miles per hour.

Full Throttle Through Chaos

There is a moment in any crash where time seems to compress and expand simultaneously. You are processing information faster than you normally would, but there is too much information to process. A car is in the air. It is above you. It is coming down. Metal is meeting metal. The sound is unlike anything else, not a single impact but a cascading series of collisions as bodywork shatters and carbon fiber disintegrates and parts scatter across the track surface.

Here is the thing that surprises people when I tell this story: I kept my foot on the throttle. Full throttle. Not because I was brave. Not because I made some calculated decision in that fraction of a second. I kept the throttle pinned because I did not know where the car that had just landed on me was going to end up. If I slowed down or braked, I might drive directly into whatever was happening in front of me. If I kept my speed up, I had a better chance of getting through the debris field and coming out the other side.

I sometimes reference Wayne Gretzky's famous line about skating to where the puck is going to be. In that moment, my version was simpler: I wanted to go where the car was not going to be. The only way to do that was to keep moving forward at speed, looking as far down the track as I could, driving through the chaos rather than stopping in the middle of it.

The Ford Mustang (the one whose right rear the McLaren had hit) spun off the track on the right side and nearly rolled over, but the driver was able to get the car stopped. My car was not so fortunate. The entire front end had been ripped off. The bodywork was destroyed. We were done. The McLaren that had caused the whole chain of events was also ultimately taken out due to damage. Three cars retired from a single moment of misjudgment. A race that had us leading in P1 ended with our car on a flatbed.

I was not injured. The safety equipment, including the five-point harness, the HANS device (Head and Neck Support, which prevents the head from snapping forward in a crash), and the reinforced cockpit structure did exactly what they were designed to do. The car absorbed the energy of the impact, and I walked away. The car itself required extensive repair, as the front end was significantly damaged, but the driver compartment remained intact. That is what good engineering looks like: not preventing the crash but ensuring survivability when the crash happens.

Car 92 in the pits at Laguna Seca after the crash in the IMSA Series. The front end was destroyed when a Ford Mustang landed on the car at over a hundred miles per hour, but the driver compartment remained intact.

My focus was entirely on driving, not taking aggressive action, just driving through the issue without creating a bigger problem. When a car lands on your hood at over a hundred miles per hour, instinct screams at you to swerve, to brake, to react. The training says: stay calm, maintain your line, let the situation develop. The data-driven mindset applies even in chaos. Do not overcorrect.

In racing, you have to process incidents as part of the sport. It was deeply disappointing. The strategy was working, the numbers were right, the execution was on track. You learn from it and you move on. The moment you let a crash define your next race, you have already lost.

The Year Before: Road America

The Laguna Seca crash was not my first experience with the violent side of motorsport. At Road America in 2018, a Porsche ahead of us experienced an electrical failure and struck us behind the rear wheel. The impact spun our

Mercedes violently into a BMW. The car required a front clip replacement – major surgery - the equivalent of rebuilding a data platform's ingestion layer from scratch.

The team worked around the clock for two weeks to get the car ready for the next race. The crash does not define the program. The recovery does.

The rebuild after Road America: cutting away the damaged front structure and welding on a replacement before reassembling the engine and drivetrain.

Two crashes in two seasons. Two cars retired. Two races where the outcome was determined not by data or strategy, but by the inherent unpredictability of putting many high-performance machines on the same piece of asphalt at the same time.

"We've All Had Data Projects Like This"

When I told the Laguna Seca story at MIT, I paused and looked around the room: "We've all had data projects like this, right?"

The laughter was immediate and knowing.

Then your CEO changes. Or there is a massive reorganization. Or budget priorities shift overnight. Or a key technology partner gets acquired and sunsets the product you have built your architecture around. I have lived through every one of these. The Ford Mustang that landed on my car did not care that we had been leading the race.

The Samsung Impact

The closest business parallel came early in my tenure as Chief Data Officer at Samsung Mobile. Two months after I started, the President who hired me was replaced. The new President had a completely different view on data. The program was quickly deprioritized – the business equivalent of having a Ford land on your hood.

Our data team had to reframe entirely, linking data projects to the new President's priorities: a music streaming service and Samsung retail stores inside Best Buy. We kept our vision down track, found the new racing line, and made the program relevant again. The underlying capability was intact. What changed was the objective.

The question is not whether your data program will have a car-goes-airborne moment. It will. The question is what you do about it.

Keep Your Vision Down Track

The single most important lesson from the Laguna Seca crash, the one that translates directly to data leadership, is this: do not fixate on the immediate obstacle.

When a car is in the air above you, every instinct tells you to stare at it. To lock your eyes on the thing that is about to hit you. This is a natural human response, and it is exactly wrong. In racing, you are taught from day one to keep your vision as far down the track as possible. Look where you want to go, not at what you want to avoid. Your hands will follow your eyes.

If you stare at the wall, you will drive into the wall. If you look through the gap, you will find the gap.

The same principle applies when your data program takes a hit. When a reorg happens, when the budget gets cut, when the executive sponsor leaves, the natural response is to fixate on the crisis. To spend every meeting talking about what went wrong. To redirect all of your energy toward the immediate problem. Some of that is necessary, of course. You cannot ignore a car that has just landed on your hood.

The leaders who recover, the ones who get the car repaired and get back on the track, are the ones who keep their vision focused on where they are going, not on what just hit them. They acknowledge the damage, assess what can be salvaged, and start working toward the next race.

Carbon Fiber Thinking

Professional motorsport has made impressive advances in safety over the past several decades. The cars we raced were equipped with head and neck restraint systems, racing harnesses, and structural reinforcements designed to protect the driver in exactly the kind of incident that happened at Laguna Seca. Carbon fiber monocoques and impact-absorbing structures are engineered to manage energy in a crash, deforming in controlled ways that dissipate force before it reaches the driver.

The tricky part is that every safety feature adds weight. In racing, weight is the enemy of performance. A heavier car is slower through the corners and harder on its brakes and tires. So the engineers who design these safety systems are constantly balancing two competing demands: protection and performance.

This is how data leaders should think about risk management and resilience in their programs. You can build a data architecture that is so heavily fortified against failure that it becomes too slow and too rigid to deliver value. You can create so many approval gates and so many layers of governance that the program becomes its own worst enemy, protected against everything but incapable of moving quickly enough to matter.

The carbon fiber approach is different. Carbon fiber is incredibly strong for its weight. It provides real protection without the performance penalty of heavier materials. The racing analogy for data programs is to build resilience that is lightweight and structural, embedded in the architecture itself rather than layered on top as bureaucratic overhead.

What does carbon fiber thinking look like in a data program? It looks like modular architecture that can absorb a change in technology without requiring a complete rebuild. It looks like governance that is automated rather than manual, so that compliance doesn't slow down delivery. It looks like distributed knowledge rather than single points of failure, making sure that the institutional understanding of your data ecosystem is not concentrated in two or three people who might leave. It looks like executive relationships that are broad rather than deep, so that the departure of a single sponsor does not collapse the entire program.

The Fatigue Factor

There is one more element of the Laguna Seca story that I have not yet emphasized, and it may be the most important one from a leadership perspective: fatigue.

By the time the restart happened, I had been driving hard for an hour. My tires were degraded, but so was I. An hour of concentration at racing speeds, managing traffic, hitting braking points, communicating with the engineer, monitoring tire condition and fuel, is physically and mentally exhausting. The heat inside a race car, even with cooling systems, is significant. The G-forces through every corner take a cumulative toll on the neck and core. The mental load of processing continuous data (car positions, closing rates, flag conditions, fuel calculations) creates a fatigue that is difficult to describe to anyone who has not experienced it.

Cooling down between stints at Watkins Glen. The heat, the G-forces, the mental load of processing continuous data at racing speeds — the fatigue is cumulative, and it is insidious.

When the yellow flag came out and our engineer asked me to survive a few more laps on the restart, I was not at my best. My reactions were slightly slower than they had been at the beginning of the stint. My judgment was marginally less sharp. My ability to process the rapidly changing situation around me at the restart was compromised by the hour of effort that had preceded it.

This is exactly what happens to data teams in organizations. Fatigue is cumulative, and it is insidious because fatigued teams do not realize how compromised they have become. A team that has been running hard for months, delivering sprint after sprint while responding to urgent requests and managing stakeholder expectations, is a team that is more likely to make mistakes when the unexpected happens. They are more likely to miss the McLaren coming from behind and more likely to make a judgment call that they would not have made when they were fresh.

Data programs rarely fail because of one catastrophic error. They fail because of the accumulation of smaller stresses – technical debt, staff turnover, scope creep, deferred maintenance – that compound until the system is brittle enough that a single unexpected event can break it.

The Convergence Problem

Catastrophic failures are almost never caused by a single variable. They are caused by convergence.

Worn tires: manageable. Low fuel: manageable. A packed restart: manageable. An amateur among professionals: manageable. Driver fatigue: manageable. All five at the same time? Each factor narrowed the margin of safety. Together, they eliminated it.

This is exactly the pattern I have observed in every major data program failure I have consulted on. Mediocre data quality, a tight budget, a leadership change, staff turnover, an aggressive timeline – each survivable alone. But in combination, the program fails.

Boardroom Translation

The Laguna Seca crash was not caused by one factor. It was caused by five manageable risks converging simultaneously. In business terms: a stretched team is survivable. A budget cut is survivable. A leadership change is survivable. A technology migration is survivable. An aggressive deadline is survivable. All five at once? That is when the Ford lands on your hood. Monitor the accumulation of risk, not just individual risks.

The Five Crashes Every CDO Will Face

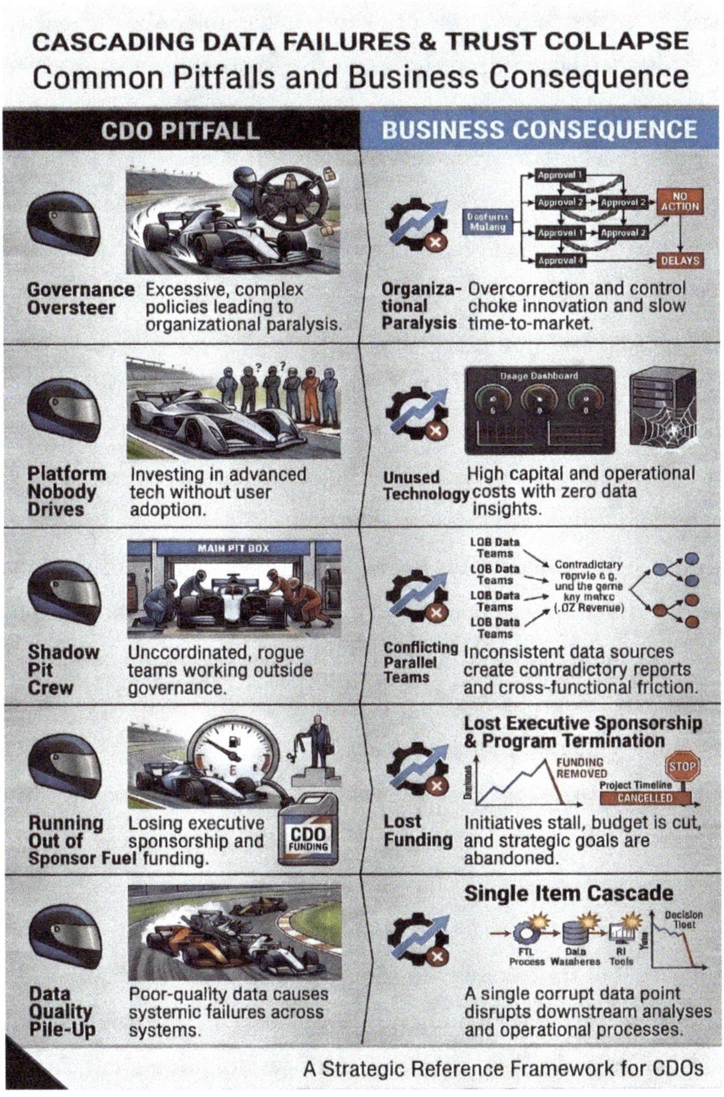

Figure 10.2: The Five Crashes Every CDO Will Face — five predictable failure patterns in data programs, each mapped to its racing equivalent.

The crashes on the racetrack are dramatic and visible. A car goes airborne. Metal meets metal at over a hundred miles per hour. Everyone sees it happen. The crashes that end data programs are quieter, slower, and often invisible until it is too late. But they follow patterns that are just as predictable as the convergence of factors at Laguna Seca. In twenty-plus years of advising data leaders, I have seen five crashes repeat themselves with remarkable consistency.

Crash 1: The Governance Oversteer. The new CDO implements governance so comprehensively it paralyzes the organization. Every request requires three approvals; every data source needs six months of onboarding. The business stops asking because the cost exceeds the value. Racing equivalent: oversteer into the wall.

Crash 2: The Platform That Nobody Drives. Tens of millions invested in a best-in-class platform. Six months after launch, utilization is below 15 percent – built for the data team, not the business users. In racing, it is a car fast in a straight line but undriveable in corners.

Crash 3: The Shadow Pit Crew. While the CDO builds the "official" platform, business units quietly build their own using departmental budgets and shadow cloud accounts. The CDO discovers this eighteen months in with no clean options. In racing, it is multiple crew members calling pit strategy independently produces chaos.

Crash 4: Running Out of Sponsor Fuel. CDO tenure averages roughly two and a half to three years[4], rarely ending because of technical failure. The executive sponsor leaves, priorities shift, and the organizational fuel quietly runs out. In racing, it is the sponsor pulled out mid-season; the car still runs, but the resources to compete are gone.

Crash 5: The Data Quality Pile-Up. Advanced analytics built on unvalidated data. Models produce results, results inform decisions, then someone discovers systematic quality issues. Every downstream decision is now suspect. The only prevention: invest in data quality before you build the models. In racing, it is a multi-car pile-up triggered by one failure.

Each of these crashes is survivable. But like the crashes at Laguna Seca and Road America, the recovery depends on honest assessment, rapid triage, and a willingness to rebuild rather than pretend the damage did not happen. The CDOs who survive are not the ones who avoid all five crashes. They are the ones who recognize the patterns early enough to brake before the impact, or who have built enough structural resilience to absorb the hit and keep racing.

The Pinhole Leak

The Laguna Seca crash taught me about the convergence of multiple factors. What happened at Spring Mountain during a sprint race weekend taught me a different lesson, one that may be even more important for data leaders: catastrophic failure does not always require multiple variables converging. Sometimes it starts with a single, almost invisible flaw.

I had qualified P2 for the sprint race and was running a solid race, chasing the leader, and finding pace I did not know I had. Then, as we neared the end, my brakes started to go soft. In the hard braking zones, I needed to pump the brake pedal to get the engagement I needed, which is not a good thing in a race car. A firm brake pedal means the hydraulic system is intact and the fluid is doing its job. A soft pedal means something is wrong, and it is getting worse with every lap.

Scott, my spotter, came over the radio and told me it was up to me: bring the car in, or hang on to the end. As a driver, you always want to see the checkered flag. You never want to park the car early. I slowed my pace and told Scott I planned to nurse the car to the finish and not take any chances. I let a couple of cars from another class pass me rather than hold them up. I did not want to push hard enough on weakening brakes to defend position.

I took the white flag, signaling one lap to go. As I rounded the halfway point of that final lap, I lost power. Scott came over the radio with words you never want to hear: "You have smoke and possible flames coming out of the back of the car. Pull over and get out."

Fire. We dress for it. We practice for it. We never want to experience it.

I pulled the car over, quickly disconnected my harness, opened the canopy, removed the steering wheel, dispatched the fire suppression system, and dove out of the car. I was out in seconds. Flames began to engulf the front and rear of the car. Smoke billowed into the sky as the carbon fiber started burning. I stood at a safe distance with no injuries whatsoever, watching the Spring Mountain safety crew descend on the scene with multiple fire extinguishers.

The chain of events that consumed my car started with a pinhole leak in a rear brake line. A tiny flaw, invisible during pre-race inspection, that allowed brake fluid to seep onto components that were already at extreme temperatures. The leak caused the progressive softening I felt in the brake pedal, the symptom I was managing during those final laps. Then the leaking fluid reached a surface hot enough to ignite it, and within seconds, a pinhole became a catastrophic fire that destroyed the car.

The view from inside the cockpit as I opened the canopy. Fire and smoke are already visible beyond the windscreen. The VBOX telemetry reads zero RPM — the car has stopped, but the fire has not.

Captured from a passing car: the KTM fully engulfed in flames. I am out of the car and at a safe distance. What started as a pinhole leak in a brake line consumed the entire machine in minutes. (Photo courtesy of Randy Wonnenberg.)

The aftermath. The charred remains of the KTM X-BOW GT2 on a flatbed. A 600-horsepower carbon fiber race car, reduced to wreckage by a flaw invisible during pre-race inspection.

One pinhole. Not a design failure. Not a convergence of five factors. A single, microscopic flaw in one component, undetectable until it was too late, that cascaded into total loss.

This is exactly the pattern I have seen destroy data programs. Not the dramatic, multi-factor convergence of Laguna Seca, but the quiet, progressive failure that starts with something so small that nobody notices it until the program is on fire.

It starts with a minor data quality issue in one source system. A single field that is not being validated correctly. A date format that is occasionally inconsistent. The issue is known. It is on a backlog somewhere. It is not considered urgent because the downstream impact appears minimal. Then the leak reaches something hot. A machine learning model is built on that data. The model goes into production. It informs decisions. Those decisions drive actions: marketing spend is reallocated, clinical trial sites are prioritized, supply chain orders are adjusted. When someone finally discovers the data quality issue, it is not just the source system that is affected. It is every model, every decision, every action downstream. The pinhole has become a fire.

I felt the brakes going soft. I knew something was wrong. I made a judgment call to nurse the car to the finish rather than pit immediately. In a data program, the equivalent is the team that notices the quality issue, acknowledges it, and decides to keep going because stopping feels like a bigger risk than continuing. Sometimes they make it. Sometimes the car catches fire with one lap to go.

The lesson is not that you should pit every time you feel something slightly off. Racing, like data leadership, requires judgment about which signals demand immediate action and which can be monitored and managed. The lesson is that small, persistent symptoms, the soft brake pedal, the data quality exception that keeps recurring, the pipeline that fails and is restarted without investigation, deserve more respect than they typically receive. A pinhole leak does not announce itself. It whispers. And if you do not listen to the whisper, you will eventually hear the explosion.

How to Recover When You Retire the Car

Not every race ends with a podium finish. Sometimes you retire the car, and the question becomes: what do you do on Monday morning?

In racing, the answer is methodical and unsentimental. Assess the damage. Determine what is repairable. Review the data. Do not assign blame. Then rebuild and get back on the track. The same framework applies to data programs.

Assess the damage honestly. Separate perception from reality. After a crash, the first reports are always worse than reality. A car that looks destroyed may have a perfectly intact drivetrain. A data program that seems dead after a reorg may have preserved its core platform and key talent. Separate the cosmetic damage from the structural damage.

Preserve what matters. After a crash, the crew immediately secures the data recorder. In a data program crisis, protect your institutional knowledge, your data assets, and your team first.

Find the new narrative. After Laguna Seca, the narrative was not "we crashed." It was "we were leading the race with a strategy that was working, and we will be back." Frame the recovery story early, and frame it honestly.

Get back on the track. The most dangerous thing a driver can do after a crash is take too long to get back in the car. The same is true of data programs. Get a version running again quickly, even if smaller in scope. Momentum is more valuable than perfection.

Underlying all four steps is a culture question: does your organization treat failure as a learning event or as a career-ending event? Recovery culture – the willingness to honestly assess failure without blame – is the prerequisite for everything else in this chapter.

Key Lesson: Setbacks are inevitable. Resilience is what determines whether you finish the race.

Business Translation: The ability to diagnose quickly, learn, and adapt separates leaders who bounce back from those who don't.

Racer Tip: Don't panic. Get the car safe, fix what you can, and get back out.

Monday Action: After a recent setback, write down the three lessons you will carry forward.

CHAPTER 11

Keep Your Eyes Up

Vision, Culture, and the Checkered Flag

The principle that helped me at Laguna Seca — keep your eyes up — turns out to be more than a survival technique. It is the single most important skill in both racing and data leadership.

When you sit in a race car and look at the road surface right in front of the hood, the way most people naturally look when they drive, everything appears to be moving incredibly fast. The pavement is a blur. The walls seem impossibly close. When you raise your vision and look out toward the next corner far down the track, something surprising happens. The world slows down. Your brain has time to process what it is seeing because you have given it a longer preview of what is coming. You are no longer reacting at the last instant. You are anticipating.

Between sessions at Watkins Glen. The ability to step back, observe, and look beyond the immediate chaos is what separates good data leaders from great ones.

This is the most important thing I can tell you about data leadership, and it is the reason I have saved it for the final chapter of this book.

The Data Quality Trap

In almost every organization I have worked with, the data team is looking at the road right in front of the car. Staring at data quality issues. Fixated on a migration. Consumed by a governance dispute. Buried in the daily operational demands of keeping pipelines running.

None of these are unimportant. But some people get so focused on the immediate problem that they lose sight of the strategic vision that justified the data program in the first place. They are so busy managing the current turn that they have no idea what the next turn looks like.

Keeping your eyes up means dealing with what is in front of you while maintaining your vision on the longer horizon. It means having the discipline to invest time in strategic planning even when operational demands are screaming for attention.

Boardroom Translation

When a driver looks at the pavement right in front of the hood, everything feels impossibly fast and reactive. When they raise their vision to the next corner far down the track, the world slows down. In business terms: the CDO who spends every hour firefighting data quality tickets and governance disputes is looking at the pavement. The CDO who blocks two hours a week for strategic thinking, even when the inbox is on fire, is looking down the track. Both are driving the same car. One of them is faster.

This is not easy. In racing, the instinct to look down is powerful and constant. You have to train yourself to override it every single lap. In data leadership, the instinct to be consumed by the immediate crisis is equally powerful. You have to train yourself, and your team, to override it every single day.

I learned this lesson from the two coaches who shaped my racing career. Alex Prémat and Cole Loftsgard have both drilled the same fundamental into me: keep your eyes up. It is the first thing a racing coach teaches, and the last thing a driver truly masters.

What It Actually Feels Like

Over the years, I have taken many people for rides in the race car at Laguna Seca, Sonoma, and Spring Mountain. The reaction is remarkably consistent. After two laps, the passenger climbs out wide-eyed: "I had no idea how violent it is. We only did two laps and I am exhausted."

They are not exaggerating. The braking compresses you against the harness, the lateral loads pin you sideways, the cockpit is brutally hot, and the cumulative toll is something you cannot appreciate from the grandstands. This is exactly how it is inside a data program. From the outside, it looks like an office job with interesting charts. The people who have never been inside a data program at full speed have no idea how intense it is.

One of the most meaningful rides happened in 2024, when I took my ninety-year-old father-in-law, John, out on the track in the KTM X-BOW GT2. John had worked for KTM's founder, Hans Trunkenpolz, in Mattighofen, Austria, in the 1950s, helping improve the company's manufacturing processes. More than seven decades later, he was strapped into the passenger seat of the latest machine to carry the KTM name, on a racetrack in the Nevada desert. From a postwar Austrian workshop to a carbon fiber race car at Spring Mountain. That is a journey that spans the full arc of what engineering, passion, and persistence can produce, and it was one of the proudest moments I have had in this sport.

Learning Czech

When I was at IBM, I lived in the Czech Republic for three years, leading Business Analytics & Optimization from Prague. I enrolled in a one-week Berlitz immersion program, determined to learn Czech. After a full week, I could basically say my name. Czech has seven grammatical cases and sounds that do not exist in English.

The best story: when I tried to speak Czech, people would politely respond, "Let's just speak English." That response is exactly what happens in organizations when you try too hard to speak the business's technical language and get it wrong – they would rather you speak plainly about data. The effort matters. The perfection does not.

What I discovered changed my approach forever: people appreciated that I tried. We would meet in the middle, with shared willingness to bridge the gap.

This is exactly what happens, or what should happen, when data leaders enter a new industry. Whether you are a data professional moving from telecommunications into pharmaceuticals, or from financial services into manufacturing, or from any industry into any other, you face a language barrier that is just as real as the one I faced in Prague.

The temptation is to walk in and immediately start speaking data. To talk about data lakes and ETL pipelines and governance frameworks. This is the equivalent of being the American who expects everyone to speak English. It is technically possible that your audience will follow along, but you have put the entire burden of translation on them, and you have signaled that you do not value their domain enough to learn even the basics of their language.

The opposite temptation is equally dangerous. Some data professionals try so hard to speak the language of the business that they abandon their own expertise entirely, becoming generalists who cannot deliver the technical depth that the organization actually needs.

The right approach is the Czech Republic approach. You try. You learn the basics of the new industry's vocabulary and its concerns. You demonstrate respect for the domain. Then, just like in Prague, you meet in the middle. The business experts recognize that they understand their domain better than you do, just as the Czech speakers recognized that they spoke English better than I spoke Czech. Together, you find a shared language that is neither pure data-speak nor pure domain-speak, but something functional and productive that both sides can use.

Scientists with a Data Problem

This lesson about translation and bridging was not merely theoretical for me. It became the foundation of how I built one of the most effective data organizations of my career.

The translators I described in Chapter 6, the "scientists with a data problem," were the Prague solution applied at enterprise scale. They bridged the gap not because they were the best technologists or the best scientists, but because they spoke both languages. The Center of Excellence delivered real impact because we had solved the translation problem.

The language gap can surface in unexpected and humbling ways. During my time at GSK, I presented regularly to the R&D Leadership Team on the progress of the information platform we were building. In the first year of the program, we had not only stood up the platform but also loaded nearly 100 percent of the structured data for analysis. I was proud of the accomplishment and eager to share it.

After one of those presentations, I was chatting with the Chief Medical Officer, and she mentioned that my repeated references to "data ingestion" had been genuinely confusing. As a physician, she heard the word "ingestion" and immediately thought of the medical meaning: a patient swallowing something. The idea of a computer platform ingesting data conjured a very different mental image than the one I intended. She paused, smiled, and asked whether, if the data loading did not go well, we referred to it as "data indigestion."

It was a small moment, but it stuck with me. From that point forward, I made a deliberate choice to say "loading" instead of "ingesting" when speaking to non-technical audiences. The technical community knows exactly what data ingestion means. The medical community hears something else entirely. That single word was creating a translation barrier I had not even noticed, and it took someone outside my domain to point it out. If you need a reminder that language differences can undermine communication even when everyone is speaking English, that is a good one.

Trust in the Cockpit and the Boardroom

Someone at my MIT presentation asked the question that cuts to the heart of everything: how do you get people to trust predictive analytics?

In racing, trust is not optional. When your engineer tells you to pit in two laps because the tire degradation model shows you are about to lose significant grip, you pit. You do not second-guess the model. You do not ask to see the data. You trust, and you act.

Race car drivers are among the most data-literate athletes in any sport. They are data geeks. There is no other sport where the athlete receives real-time data feeds during competition to the same degree. An NFL quarterback does not have a dashboard showing defensive alignment probabilities. A race car driver has a dashboard full of data, an engineer feeding information through the radio, and a strategy being continuously recalculated based on what the data is showing.

The lesson is not that everyone needs a heads-up display. It is that trust is built through experience and demonstrated value, not through mandates or governance policies. Race car drivers trust their data because they have seen, lap after lap, that the data makes them faster. When the tire model says you are losing grip, and you can feel it through the steering wheel, and the new tires are transformationally better – that builds trust. The data matched reality.

In organizations, trust breaks down when the data does not match reality. Building trust requires closing those gaps, and it requires patience, because trust is earned over time, not installed overnight.

At GSK, building trust required letting the scientists lead the narrative. The translator model (scientists who understood data) was essential. In genetics, for instance, one of the scientists working within our Center of Excellence published a paper demonstrating that drug programs supported by genetic evidence were two to three times more likely to ultimately become approved drugs compared to programs without such evidence[5]. That finding did not come from the data platform team making claims about science. It came from a credentialed scientist using the data platform to generate an insight that changed how the organization prioritized its pipeline.

The Cultural Shift

Everything in this book depends on one thing that cannot be engineered or purchased: culture.

A data-driven culture is not a culture where everyone has access to dashboards. It is a culture where people trust data enough to act on it. Where the driver pits when the model says to pit, not two laps later when the tires are already gone. Where the business leader changes course when the analysis shows the current path is not working, even when that analysis contradicts their intuition.

The Checkered Flag

In racing, the checkered flag is also a beginning. The moment the race ends, the work of preparing for the next race begins. The data is downloaded, the telemetry analyzed, the strategy dissected. The team does not celebrate for long, and they do not mourn for long. The next race is coming.

I started this book by walking into a room at MIT wearing a racing suit. Not a costume, but a suit that had been worn in competition, that had been in the car when the Ford Mustang landed on us and when the Porsche spun us into the BMW. A suit with some miles on it.

The data is clear. The telemetry supports the thesis. The lap times prove the concept.

Now it is your turn to drive.

Keep your eyes up. Stay on the throttle. Go find your checkered flag.

On the GT4 podium at Watkins Glen International in the SRO GT4 Series. The checkered flag — and the green flag for the next race.

After a race win at Spring Mountain. The work is never done, but some moments are worth savoring. (Photo courtesy of Spring Mountain Motor Resort and Country Club.)

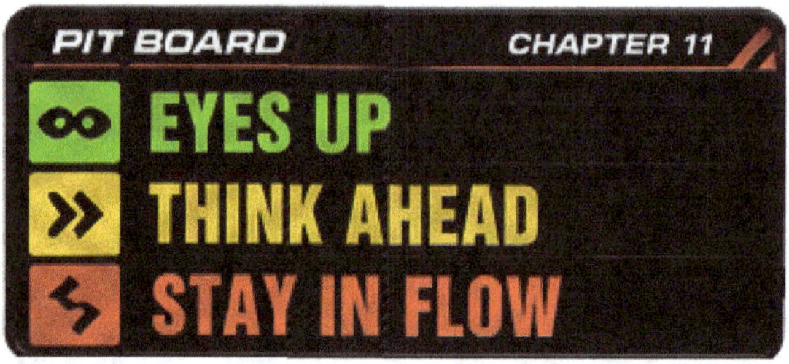

Key Lesson: Great drivers look beyond the next turn. Vision and anticipation create time and options.

Business Translation: Leaders who anticipate change position their organizations to adapt, rather than react.

Racer Tip: Look through the corner, not at it. Focus on where you want to go.

Monday Action: Identify one upcoming change or disruption and plan one move you can make now.

CHAPTER 12

The Next Lap

The Future of Data Leadership

The race is over. The data has been downloaded, the telemetry reviewed, the strategy dissected. And then someone asks the question that separates teams that compete from teams that win: What's next?

The Race Engineer in Your Pocket

In Chapter 3, we explored how AI and human judgment work together in racing, the driver processing what the car feels, the engineer processing what the data shows, and the best decisions emerging from the combination. The next evolution of this partnership is already taking shape, and it is more profound than most people realize.

AI copilots are becoming the race engineer that every data leader has always wanted but could never afford.

Consider what a world-class race engineer does during a race. They are monitoring dozens of data streams simultaneously: tire degradation curves, fuel consumption rates, weather radar, competitor gaps, pit window calculations. They synthesize all of that into a single clear instruction delivered to the driver at exactly the right moment. "Pit this lap." "Push for two more laps." "Save fuel, we're going long." The driver does not need to understand the hundred calculations behind the call. They need the call.

AI-powered decision support is heading in the same direction for data leaders and business executives. Not AI making the decision, but AI doing the synthesis that a human could not do alone, across more data sources, at greater speed, with a consistency that no human team can sustain over a twelve-hour race or a twelve-month strategy cycle. The emerging generation of AI copilots can monitor your data pipelines, flag anomalies before they cascade, draft analyses of incoming data, and present options in a format that lets a human make the actual call.

Formula 1 is already living this with its hybrid approach to intelligence. The cars run hybrid power units, combining internal combustion with electrical energy recovery. The teams run hybrid intelligence, combining human expertise with algorithmic analysis. The sport has not replaced engineers with software. It has given engineers better tools, and the engineers have become more effective as a result.

This is the future for every organization. Not artificial intelligence replacing data leaders. AI as the ultimate race engineer, providing real-time decision support at a scale that no human team could match alone. The driver stays in the car. The engineer stays on the radio. The AI handles the calculations that would take a team of analysts hours to assemble, and delivers them in seconds.

The next evolution is already taking shape. Agentic AI systems – autonomous agents that can not only analyze data but take action on it – are moving from research into production. Imagine a race engineer who does not just tell you the tire degradation model suggests pitting in two laps, but who has already radioed the pit crew, confirmed the tire allocation, and calculated the fuel load for the next stint before you even respond. In the data world, this means AI agents that can autonomously rerun a failed Extract, Transform, and Load (ETL) pipeline, open a data-quality ticket when anomaly detection flags an issue, draft a first-cut root-cause analysis for the on-call engineer, or pre-stage a data refresh ahead of a scheduled board report. The human still makes the strategic calls – when to pit, which tires to run, whether to change the race strategy entirely. But the low-risk, high-frequency operational decisions happen at machine speed, freeing the human to focus on the decisions that actually require judgment. The organizations building this capability today are the ones that will have a decisive advantage when agentic AI matures from experimental to essential, which, based on the current trajectory, is not a matter of years but of quarters.

The Sizzle and the Steak: AI for Data Preparation

There is an enormous, overlooked opportunity that most organizations are missing. When people talk about AI in business, they talk about the sizzle: predicting churn, optimizing pricing, detecting fraud. Those applications are valuable. But the highest-return use of AI may be on the data itself – not making business decisions, but preparing the data for decisions. Curating it, standardizing it, cleaning it, linking it.

Data scientists spend sixty to eighty percent of their time cleaning and preparing data. Much of that work could be augmented by the same machine learning techniques we apply to business problems. If you could use AI to detect and resolve data quality issues, standardize formats across disparate sources, and link records across systems, you would improve the foundation on which every business decision rests. The business decision model is only as good as the data that feeds it. Improving the preparation layer has a multiplicative effect on every downstream application.

In practice, this means Natural Language Processing (NLP) for entity extraction from unstructured documents, a capability that +tellic built for pharmaceutical clients, transforming millions of publications into structured, queryable knowledge. It means machine-learning-based data matching across sources, where Stonebraker's Tamr has demonstrated real effectiveness at resolving entities across messy datasets at enterprise scale. Large language models have accelerated this dramatically. Tasks that once required months of custom NLP development can now be accomplished with generative AI systems that understand context and nuance. Natural language interfaces let business users query data in plain English rather than writing SQL. But a generative AI system is only as good as the data it queries. The foundation still matters. Generative AI raises the stakes on getting it right. This is not glamorous work. It is the highest-return investment most data leaders are not making.

Boardroom Translation

A race engineer does not just call pit strategy — they also calibrate the sensors, validate the telemetry feeds, and make sure the data reaching the driver is clean and trustworthy. In business terms: before you invest in the AI that makes decisions, invest in the AI that prepares your data for decisions. The sizzle is worthless if the steak is raw.

The AI Adoption Spectrum

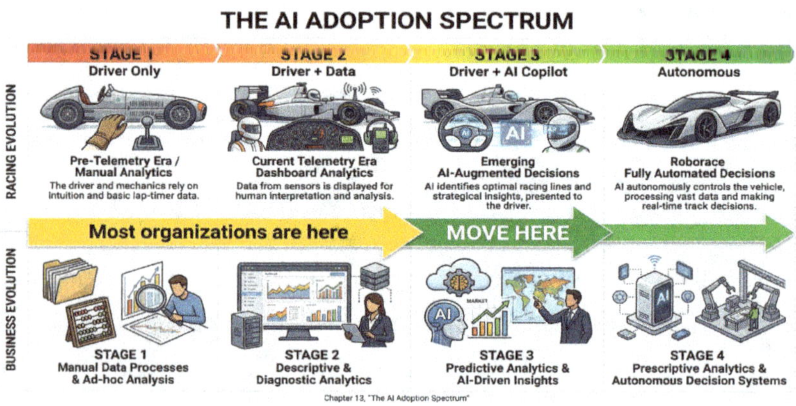

Figure 12.1: The AI Adoption Spectrum — from driver-only to fully autonomous, mapped to the evolution of AI in business decision-making.

AI governance is the safety equipment, not the bureaucracy. The FIA does not write technical regulations to slow Formula 1 cars down. It writes them to ensure the competition is safe enough to actually happen. AI governance works the same way. Model validation, bias detection, and explainability requirements are the safety equipment that lets you push harder with confidence. Set the technical regulations. Then let the teams go fast.

The distance between question and answer is collapsing. Large language models are dismantling the bottleneck between a business user's natural-language question and a structured data answer. The analyst still interprets and validates. But the distance from question to useful answer has collapsed from days to seconds.

Where is your organization on the trust spectrum? Imagine a spectrum from fully manual to fully autonomous. At one end: the pre-telemetry era, the driver alone. In the middle: human intuition continuously calibrated by analytical inputs. Moving further: the driver plus an AI copilot. At the far end: fully autonomous. Most organizations are still in the driver-plus-data phase. The goal is to reach driver-plus-AI-copilot, and trust has to be built the same way it was built for data – through demonstrated reliability over time.

Getting there requires four investments, mapping directly to the four-resource framework from Chapter 5. *People:* AI literacy cannot be confined to the data team. *Data:* garbage-in, garbage-out does not disappear with generative AI – it accelerates. A large language model querying a data swamp produces confident-sounding nonsense at scale. *Infrastructure:* AI workloads are computationally different from traditional analytics. *Decisions:* decision rights around AI-assisted versus human decisions need to be explicit.

Knowing When to Keep Your Hands on the Wheel

The critical question is not whether to automate, but what to automate. Fraud detection, supply chain optimization, dynamic pricing – automate these aggressively. But strategic decisions require judgment under genuine uncertainty: incomplete information, competing values, consequences that ripple for years. The organizations that figure out which decisions belong in which category will have a decisive advantage.

The Democratization of Speed

The tools that once required massive investment have been democratized. MoTeC's i2 Pro is free. Cloud platforms have eliminated upfront infrastructure costs. Natural language interfaces let business users query data without writing SQL. The competitive advantage has shifted from having the tools to knowing how to use them, from having data to having the culture that acts on data. A mid-sized manufacturer with a smart data strategy can now rival what only Fortune 100 companies could afford five years ago. The car matters, but the driver matters more.

Racing to Business: A Quick Reference

Throughout this book, I have drawn parallels between racing concepts and business challenges. The following table brings the most important of those connections together in one place. Consider it a pit board for the rest of your career.

Racing Concept	Business Equivalent	Key Lesson
Trail Braking	Resource Allocation in Projects	Transfer "grip" smoothly from planning to execution; releasing one input while increasing another avoids understeer (delays) and oversteer (chaos)
Late Apex	Strategic Pivots	Sacrifice short-term speed for long-term acceleration; invest in data quality now for faster insights later
Tire Degradation	Team Burnout and Technical Debt	Performance does not degrade linearly; monitor cumulative stress because the cliff edge arrives without warning
Pit Stop Timing	Platform Migrations and Reorgs	The cost of stopping is real, but the cost of not stopping is worse; time the change, do not avoid it
Fuel Management	Budget and Capital Allocation	Predictable depletion requires planning; running out ends the race regardless of how fast you were
Weather Prediction	Competitive and Market Intelligence	Build your own models rather than relying on the same forecasts as every competitor
Telemetry Overlay	Performance Benchmarking	Compare your execution against the best, corner by corner, metric by metric
Safety Car Restart	Post-Crisis Recovery	How you restart after a disruption determines the next phase; the crisis itself is already behind you
The Perfect Lap	Operational Excellence	No single corner wins the race; consistent execution across every element, compounded over time, is what separates winners from the field

The Grid

I want to close this book where every race begins: on the starting grid.

It is five minutes before the green flag. I am strapped into the KTM X-BOW GT2, the harness pulled tight across my chest and shoulders, the HANS device secured, the helmet visor down. The car is rolling behind the pace car, the sequential gearbox in first, the field lined up in their assigned positions based on qualifying.

Green, green, green....the Sportscar Series race starts under the Michelin bridge on the Lauda C North/South course at Spring Mountain (Photo courtesy of Spring Mountain Motor Resort and Country Club.)

I can hear engines at different pitches, feel the vibration of my own car through the seat, smell the mix of race fuel and hot brakes that defines this moment.

The data is loaded. Tire pressures set from predictive models, adjusted for today's track temperature. Fuel calculated to the fraction of a gallon, with a strategy that accounts for two planned pit stops and one unplanned caution period, because there is always an unplanned caution period. Brake bias dialed to the setting that yesterday's qualifying telemetry confirmed as optimal.

The strategy draws on everything this book has discussed. We have decomposed the race into its component segments. We have modeled our resource consumption. We have studied the external intelligence and reviewed the historical patterns. We have prepared for failure. And my eyes are up, looking through the windscreen to the first braking zone.

My engineer's voice comes through the radio, calm, clear, and direct. "Pace car coming in this lap. Make sure you are in first gear, keep the revs up, and hold fifty until the green. Have a good race."

Everything converges in this moment. The data, the strategy, the people, the culture of trust that lets a driver act on an engineer's call without hesitation. This is what a data-driven organization looks like when it is working. Not the dashboards. Not the platforms. The moment when a human being, supported by data and surrounded by a team that has done the work, makes a decision and commits to it fully.

The green flag drops. I go to full throttle.

Before I started racing, data was something I worked with. I respected it. I built systems around it. But there was always a distance between me and the data – the comfortable distance of a conference room and a review cycle. After I strapped into a car and felt the consequences of analytical decisions, that distance collapsed. Data became something I believed in, the way a pilot believes in instruments when the clouds close in and the ground disappears.

You cannot debate a lap time. You cannot argue with the stopwatch. Either you found the tenth of a second, or you did not.

When the moment of truth arrives, data is what remains.

With the crew after a race win at Spring Mountain. The race is not won by the driver alone — it is won by the entire system, operating in concert. Sigier Motorsport team (left to right): Max Putze, Scott Budshaw, Simon Sigier, Mark, Will Knox, David Moreno. (Photo courtesy of Spring Mountain Motor Resort and Country Club.)

On the podium at Spring Mountain with Kha Phan (third) and Jeff Frazer (second), all competing in KTM X-BOW GT2 race cars. The competition pushes everyone to be better. (Photo courtesy of Spring Mountain Motor Resort and Country Club.)

Key Lesson: The race never really ends. Continuous improvement and teamwork compound over time.

Business Translation: A culture of learning, iteration, and shared purpose drives long-term results.

Racer Tip: Celebrate the win, then reset. The next lap is the most important one.

Monday Action: Recognize one teammate this week who made your team better.

Appendix: Racing Glossary for Non-Racers

If you picked up this book from the business shelf and found yourself in unfamiliar territory when the conversation turned to apexes and tire compounds, this glossary is for you. These terms appear throughout the book and are defined here for quick reference.

Apex – The point in a corner where the car passes closest to the inside edge of the track. Hitting the apex correctly determines your exit speed and therefore your speed down the following straight.

Late apex – A racing technique where the driver delays the apex point past the geometric midpoint of the corner, sacrificing mid-corner speed to gain a better exit angle and earlier throttle application. Counterintuitive but faster.

Trail braking – The technique of gradually releasing brake pressure while simultaneously increasing steering input as the car transitions from braking into cornering. The most important technique in road racing, and the one that separates fast drivers from faster ones.

Understeer – When the front tires lose traction and the car pushes wide of the intended line, refusing to turn as sharply as the driver commands. Often described as the car "plowing" or "pushing."

Oversteer – When the rear tires lose traction and the back of the car swings wide. The car rotates more than the driver intends. Dramatic to watch, terrifying to experience at speed.

Contact patch – The small area of each tire that is actually touching the road surface at any given moment. Roughly the size of a postcard, and responsible for all braking, cornering, and acceleration grip.

Grip budget – The finite amount of traction available from a tire at any moment. The driver can spend that budget on braking or cornering, but not both at full demand simultaneously. Exceed the budget and the tire slides.

Weight transfer – The shift of a car's mass under acceleration, braking, or cornering. Braking transfers weight forward (loading the front tires); acceleration transfers it rearward. Managing weight transfer is fundamental to fast, controlled driving.

Sector times – The lap divided into timed segments between fixed points on the circuit. Sector analysis reveals exactly where a driver is gaining or losing time, turning a single lap time into an actionable breakdown.

Pit window – The range of laps during which pitting for fuel, tires, or a driver change is strategically optimal. Missing the window can cost positions or force a suboptimal second stop.

Tire degradation – The progressive loss of grip as a tire wears through use. Degradation is nonlinear: tires perform well until they reach a threshold, then grip falls off sharply – "the cliff."

Endurance racing – Racing formats lasting two hours or longer, requiring management of fuel, tires, car health, and driver fatigue over extended periods. Multiple drivers typically share the car.

Qualifying – A timed session before the race that determines each car's starting position on the grid. Fastest qualifier starts first ("on pole").

Telemetry – Data transmitted from sensors on the car to the engineering team, covering speed, throttle position, brake pressure, tire temperatures, engine parameters, and more. The raw material of racing data analysis.

Speed trace – A graph plotting vehicle speed against track position or time. Overlaying two speed traces reveals exactly where one lap is faster or slower than another.

Appendix: For the Racing Reader

If you picked up this book because you are a racer, or because you want to be one, this section is for you. Throughout the book, I have used motorsports to illuminate data and analytics principles. But I know some of you read it the other way around: you came for the racing and stayed for the data. That is perfectly fine. In fact, that is how it happened for me, too.

What follows is a practical guide to help you go deeper. Whether you're a club racer looking to shave a second off your lap time, someone who just signed up for your first track day, or a weekend warrior who wants to understand what all those squiggly lines on the telemetry screen actually mean, this appendix will point you in the right direction.

Getting Started with Telemetry Analysis

The single best thing you can do to get faster is to start logging data. You do not need a Formula 1 budget. You do not even need to spend more than a few hundred dollars. Here are three options at different price points:

Phone-based entry point: Harry's LapTimer ($30-$40). If you are just getting started, Harry's LapTimer turns your smartphone into a surprisingly capable data logger. Mount your phone in the car (securely, please), and it will record GPS-based lap times, speed traces, lateral G-forces, and more. It will not give you the precision of a dedicated unit, but it is an outstanding way to learn what telemetry analysis looks like before you invest serious money.

Mid-range: RaceCapture by Autosport Labs ($400-$800). RaceCapture offers configurable data logging with OBD-II integration, GPS tracking, and the ability to add external sensors for things like brake pressure and suspension travel. The accompanying software is solid, and the community around it is active and helpful. It is a great step up when you are ready to get serious.

Professional-grade: AiM Solo 2 DL ($900-$1,000). The AiM Solo 2 is the standard in club racing for good reason. It is reliable, accurate, and integrates cleanly with AiM's Race Studio analysis software. The DL version connects to your car's ECU for additional data channels. If you plan to race competitively, this is the unit most of your competitors will be running, which makes data sharing and comparison much easier.

Once you have a data logger, you will need software to analyze what it captures. The good news is that some of the best options are free:

- **AiM Race Studio 3** is free with AiM hardware and provides excellent lap comparison, channel analysis, and track mapping tools.
- **MoTeC i2** is free to download and is arguably the most powerful telemetry analysis software available at any price. The learning curve is steep, but the capability is extraordinary. Many professional teams use it.
- **Harry's LapTimer** includes its own analysis tools right on your phone, which is perfect for reviewing sessions trackside between runs.

Now, what should you actually look at? When you are staring at your first data download, it is easy to feel overwhelmed. Start with three things:

1. **Brake points.** Where exactly are you getting on the brakes for each corner? Are you consistent lap to lap? As we discussed in Chapter 2, braking is where the biggest time gains hide.

2. **Throttle application.** How smoothly and how early are you getting back to full throttle on corner exit? Hesitation here costs you time all the way down the next straight.
3. **Minimum corner speed.** This is the slowest point in each corner. If your minimum speed is lower than it should be, you are probably braking too much or turning in at the wrong point.

The technique I described in Chapter 2, overlaying your lap data against a faster driver's data on the same track, is the most powerful learning tool in racing. When you can see exactly where another driver is carrying more speed, braking later, or getting to throttle sooner, the abstract goal of "go faster" becomes a concrete set of specific actions. Find someone at your track days or race weekends who is a second or two quicker and ask if they will share their data. Most racers will say yes. It is one of the best traditions in the sport.

Racing Schools and Series Mentioned in This Book

If you are looking to get started, a racing school is the best investment you can make. Several that shaped my own journey or come highly recommended:

- **Radford Racing School** (formerly Bob Bondurant Racing School), Phoenix, AZ. This is where I first learned road racing in 2012. The multi-day programs take you from fundamentals through high-performance driving, and some programs put you in open-wheel formula cars. It is an unforgettable experience.
- **Exotics Racing**, Las Vegas, NV. This is where I began wheel-to-wheel racing in French Mitjet race cars early in my career. They no longer offer the competitive racing series where I got my start, but they still provide supercar and racecar driving experiences that are a great introduction to high-performance driving.
- **Porsche Track Experience**, Birmingham, AL. The experience puts you behind the wheel of the latest Porsche lineup on a

purpose-built track. The instruction is excellent, and you get to feel what a properly engineered sports car can do in a controlled, professional environment.

- **Skip Barber Racing School**, Sebring, FL. One of the most storied names in American racing instruction. Their programs range from introductory driving experiences to multi-day racing schools, and they have produced generations of competitive drivers. If you are serious about learning racecraft, Skip Barber is a name you should know.

The professional series featured in this book include:

- **IMSA Michelin Pilot Challenge**, where Big Data in Action competed in 2018 and 2019 in multi-class endurance races at tracks including Daytona International Speedway.
- **SRO GT4 Americas**, a competitive GT series with professional and am-level drivers sharing the grid.
- **Spring Mountain Sportscar Series**, based at Spring Mountain Motor Resort and Country Club in Pahrump, Nevada. This is where you will find me most months for a race weekend. The facility's famous Charleston Peak circuit is the longest road course in the United States and the second longest in the world by the facility's measure, behind only the Nürburgring Nordschleife in Germany. The series attracts a competitive field of dedicated amateur and semi-professional drivers, and the sheer length of the track makes it one of the most demanding and rewarding circuits anywhere.
- **NASA (National Auto Sport Association) endurance racing**, including the grueling 6-hour format at Utah Motorsports Campus.

If you are thinking about getting on track yourself, know that you do not have to jump straight into professional racing. Many regions across the country have SCCA (Sports Car Club of America) and NASA chapters that offer affordable High Performance Driving Events (HPDEs), time trials, and club racing. These organizations provide structured learning environments with experienced instructors, and annual competition licenses are surprisingly affordable. You will find racers at every level, from first-timers to seasoned veterans, and the community is welcoming. Start with an HPDE day. You will be hooked.

Recommended Reading and Watching

Books

- *Going Faster! Mastering the Art of Race Driving* by Carl Lopez. This is the Skip Barber Racing School's official manual, and it is the best single volume on the fundamentals of race driving. If you only read one book on driving technique, make it this one.
- *Speed Secrets: Professional Race Driving Techniques* by Ross Bentley. Bentley's approach is thoughtful and systematic, and his focus on the mental side of performance driving is invaluable. He has written several follow-up volumes, all worth your time.
- *Data Power: Using Racecar Data Acquisition* by Buddy Fey. This is the book specifically about racing data analysis. If the telemetry discussion in Chapter 2 sparked your interest, Fey's book will take you much deeper into how to read and interpret the data your car is generating.

Films and Series

Several films and series referenced in this book capture different facets of the racing world:

- *Ford v Ferrari*, for its portrayal of the relentless pursuit of the perfect lap.
- *Rush*, for the rivalry between Lauda's data-driven approach and Hunt's instinct.
- *Senna*, Asif Kapadia's documentary about the transcendent Ayrton Senna.

- *Gran Turismo*, the unlikely story of a sim racer who made it to Le Mans.
- *F1*, the feature film that brought the spectacle of Formula 1 to mainstream cinema.
- *Drive to Survive*, the series that changed how the world sees Formula 1.

Online Resources

For telemetry analysis tutorials, I would encourage you to search YouTube for racing data analysis walkthroughs. The community has produced excellent content covering everything from basic speed trace interpretation to advanced techniques in MoTeC and AiM software. The quality of freely available instructional material today would have been unimaginable when I started racing.

Appendix: Business Reader's Quick Start

Applying the Five Racing Principles in Five Weeks

The principles in this book are not theoretical. They are actionable, and you can begin applying them immediately. Here is a five-week plan to put them to work in your organization.

Week 1: Decompose One Key Metric (Principle 1)

Pick your organization's single most important metric: revenue, churn, time-to-market, patient enrollment, whatever your leadership watches most closely. Break it into five to seven sub-components, the way a driver breaks a corner into braking, trail braking, turn-in, apex, exit, and acceleration. For each sub-component, identify the leading indicator that would tell you whether performance is improving or degrading before the headline metric moves. The sub-component with the most variance is where the time is hiding.

Week 2: Map Your Four Resources (Principle 2)

List the four resource categories that sustain your program: budget and capital, people and capacity, technology and infrastructure, and leadership attention. For each one, assess the current level, the depletion rate, and whether there is a cliff-edge risk, a point where performance degrades suddenly rather than gradually. Identify which resource will run out first at the current burn rate. That is your tire degradation problem, and it needs a pit stop strategy before it becomes a crisis.

Week 3: Audit Your External Data (Principle 3)

List every external data source your organization currently uses for decision-making. Then identify three decisions that could be improved with data you do not currently have. Research whether that data exists in the public domain, through commercial providers, or within your partner ecosystem. The goal is not to acquire everything at once. The goal is to identify the weather model that your competitors are not building.

Week 4: Look Sideways for Unique Sources (Principle 4)

Identify an adjacent industry that solves a problem similar to yours using different data. Banks know things about consumer behavior that retailers do not. Shipping companies know things about supply chains that manufacturers do not. Contact one person in that adjacent industry and ask what data they rely on for their version of your challenge. Evaluate whether their data sources could apply to your domain. As Chapter 8 showed, the most valuable source may be one that another industry collects without ever realizing what it is worth to you.

Week 5: Mine Your Archives (Principle 5)

Pull three years of historical data on your key metric and its sub-components. Look for the white space: what did not happen that should have? Where are the gaps between events? Build one simple predictive model using historical patterns to forecast next quarter's performance. The goal is not a perfect model. The goal is to start treating your historical data as a laboratory rather than a museum, and to find the one insight that everyone else missed because they were too busy staring at the present.

After five weeks, you will have a decomposed view of your most important metric, a resource map that identifies your biggest vulnerability, an inventory of external data opportunities, at least one cross-industry insight, and a historical model that predicts what comes next. That is a pit board for your data program. Use it.

Acknowledgments

No one builds a racing program alone, and no one writes a book alone either.

My deepest thanks to Trina, for living every lap with me and for the grace to let me chase something that made no sense on paper but made every kind of sense in the heart. She was in the grandstands at Laguna Seca the day the Ford Mustang landed on our car going into the Corkscrew. She heard the announcers describe a crash involving Car 92 and had no way of knowing whether I was hurt, whether I was walking, whether I was conscious. She lived that moment, and she came back to the next race. That is a kind of courage that deserves its own chapter.

To my father, Dean, who taught me how to work on cars, starting with the Dodge Coronet R/T in the back garage. He was my first pit crew and towed me home many times after breaking the car on the drag strip. Dad attended my first IMSA race at Daytona and was in awe of the circus around him. He does not understand why his adult son is driven to race but is still supportive.

To my father-in-law, John, whose early career at KTM in Austria planted a seed that bloomed seven decades later into a carbon fiber race car in the Nevada desert. That ride together at Spring Mountain is one of the proudest moments of my racing life.

To Alexandre Prémat, my professional racing coach from 2016 to 2020, whose precision behind the wheel taught me that feel without data is guessing and data without feel is arithmetic.

To Cole Loftsgard, my coach since 2022, whose relentless focus on fundamentals continues to push me forward. Cole & I have spent many hours looking at data and video to push the KTM faster.

To Simon Sigier, who started as a mechanic on the Big Data in Action crew in 2018, became Crew Chief in 2019, and after the pandemic launched Sigier Motorsport to provide team management and trackside services focused exclusively on the KTM. Simon is the go-to guy for racing KTMs in the United States, and he and I have lived this journey together. Every chapter of this book has a piece of Simon in it.

To the crew and engineers who kept Car 92 and Car 592 on the track, often through long nights and impossible timelines, particularly after the crashes at Road America and Laguna Seca and the fire at Spring Mountain. Your commitment to rebuilding and returning to competition embodies the resilience this book champions.

To Spring Mountain Motor Resort and Country Club, that provides a world class racing facility, employees and a track services team that is second to none. It has been a pleasure to race in the Sportscar Series over the past 3 years and I look forward to the next season.

To Dr. Richard Y. Wang, for two decades of leadership through the MIT CDOIQ Symposium. The community you have built gave this book its first audience and its intellectual home.

To my colleagues at GlaxoSmithKline, Samsung, and IBM, who trusted me to build data organizations at scale and who taught me, through both victories and failures, the lessons that fill these pages. The translators, the scientists with a data problem, the engineers who kept the pipelines running at three in the morning: you know who you are, and you have my lasting respect.

To the technology partners whose platforms powered the Big Data in Action program and my work across industries: Modak, +tellic, Tamr, and Cloudera. Your contributions to the practice of data management are woven throughout this book.

To every data leader, CDO, and analytics professional who sat in the audience at a conference and leaned forward when I walked out in a racing suit. Your response told me this was a book worth writing.

And to every racer who has ever sat in a trailer after a session, staring at a speed trace, looking for the tenth of a second that separates good from great. This book is for you, too.

References and Sources

Statistics References

1. On the F1 pit-stop deep-learning model reporting 92.31 percent recall: see Abhijai Sasikumar, A. Anny Leema, and P. Balakrishnan, "Data-Driven Pit Stop Decision Support for Formula 1 Using Deep Learning Models," *Frontiers in Artificial Intelligence* 8 (2025): article 1673148, https://doi.org/10.3389/frai.2025.1673148. The 70.59 percent accuracy and 92.31 percent recall figures correspond to the model's evaluation on 2025 Chinese Grand Prix data.

2. The widely cited figure that roughly 85 percent of big data and analytics projects fail to deliver on their objectives traces to Gartner analyst commentary and has been echoed across industry reporting, including Randy Bean and Thomas H. Davenport, "Companies Are Failing in Their Efforts to Become Data-Driven," *Harvard Business Review*, February 5, 2019, and subsequent NewVantage Partners *Data and AI Leadership Executive Survey* editions. Estimates across sources range from roughly 60 to 87 percent depending on how "success" is defined; the figure should be read as directional.

3. On the roughly six-to-one gap in AI success likelihood between organizations with strong data integration and literacy and those without: see NewVantage Partners, *Data and AI Leadership Executive Survey 2023* (Boston: NewVantage Partners, 2023); see also Sam Ransbotham et al., "Expanding AI's Impact with Organizational Learning," *MIT Sloan*

Management Review and Boston Consulting Group, October 2020, which reports that organizations combining multiple modes of human-AI learning are about six times more likely to realize significant financial benefits from AI.

4. Average Chief Data Officer tenure of roughly two and a half to three years is reported consistently in Gartner and IDC analyst commentary from 2020 through 2024; see also Randy Bean and Thomas H. Davenport, "Why Do Chief Data Officers Have Such Short Tenures?," *Harvard Business Review*, August 2021, and Bean's *Fail Fast, Learn Faster* (Hoboken, NJ: Wiley, 2021).

5. Matthew R. Nelson et al., "The Support of Human Genetic Evidence for Approved Drug Indications," *Nature Genetics* 47, no. 8 (August 2015): 856–60.

Primary Source

- Ramsey, Mark, Ph.D. "Big Data in Action: Using Data for Professional Auto Racing." Presentation at the MIT CDOIQ Symposium.

Formula 1 and Data Analytics

- Amazon Web Services. "F1 Insights Powered by AWS." aws.amazon.com/sports/f1/
- Amazon Web Services. "Formula 1 Case Study." aws.amazon.com/solutions/case-studies/formula-one/
- Amazon Web Services. "Real-Time Storytelling: The AWS Architecture Behind Formula 1 Track Pulse." AWS Media Blog, 2025.
- Formula One World Championship Limited. "Formula 1 and AWS Launch 'Real-Time Race Track' Experience." corp.formula1.com, 2025.

- Frontiers in Artificial Intelligence. "Data-Driven Pit Stop Decision Support for Formula 1 Using Deep Learning Models." frontiersin.org, 2025.
- Catapult Sports. "How Data Analysis Transforms F1 Race Performance." catapult.com/blog, 2025.

Motorsports Technology

- MoTeC. "i2 Data Analysis Software." motec.com.au/i2/i2overview/
- KTM. "X-BOW GT2." ktm.com/en-us/models/x-bow/x-bow-gt2-2020.html
- Wikipedia. "Alexandre Prémat." en.wikipedia.org/wiki/Alexandre_Prémat

Film References

- *F1.* Directed by Joseph Kosinski. Apple Original Films, 2025.
- *Ford v Ferrari.* Directed by James Mangold. 20th Century Fox, 2019.
- *Rush.* Directed by Ron Howard. Universal Pictures, 2013.
- *Senna.* Directed by Asif Kapadia. Universal Pictures, 2010.
- *Gran Turismo.* Directed by Neill Blomkamp. Sony Pictures, 2023.
- *Formula 1: Drive to Survive.* Netflix, Seasons 1-6, 2019-2024.

Data Management, Analytics, and Industry Research

- Bean, Randy. *Data and AI Leadership: Visionary Data Strategy for Enterprise AI Futures.* Wiley, 2024.
- Bean, Randy. *Fail Fast, Learn Faster.* Wiley, 2021.
- Bhandari, Inderpal, Edward Colet, Jennifer Parker, Zachary Pines, Rajiv Pratap, and Krishnakumar Ramanujam. "Advanced Scout:

Data Mining and Knowledge Discovery in NBA Data." *Data Mining and Knowledge Discovery,* 1, 121–125 (1997). IBM T.J. Watson Research Center.

- Davenport, Thomas H. *The AI Advantage: How to Put the Artificial Intelligence Revolution to Work.* MIT Press, 2018.
- Davenport, Thomas H. and Randy Bean. *All-In on AI: How Smart Companies Win Big with Artificial Intelligence.* Harvard Business Review Press, 2023.
- Davenport, Thomas H. and Jeanne G. Harris. *Competing on Analytics.* Harvard Business Review Press, 2007/2017.
- Lewis, Michael. *Moneyball.* W. W. Norton & Company, 2003.
- Mason, Hilary and DJ Patil. *Data Driven: Creating a Data Culture.* O'Reilly Media, 2015.
- O'Neil, Cathy. *Weapons of Math Destruction: How Big Data Increases Inequality and Threatens Democracy.* Crown, 2016.
- Redman, Thomas C. *Data Driven: Profiting from Your Most Important Business Asset.* Harvard Business Review Press, 2008.
- Redman, Thomas C. *Getting in Front on Data: Who Does What.* Technics Publications, 2016.
- Stonebraker, Michael. Research on data integration and "after-the-fact" data mastering. MIT CSAIL.
- Wang, Richard Y. *Journey to Data Quality.* MIT Press, 2006.
- U.S. Food and Drug Administration. "Center for Real-World Evidence Innovation." FDA.gov, December 2024.
- Tamr, Inc. AI-driven data mastering and entity resolution. tamr.com.
- +tellic. NLP and entity extraction for pharmaceutical data. tellic.com.
- Modak. Nabu dynamic Spark pipeline technology. modak.com.
- Cloudera. Cloudera Data Platform (CDP). cloudera.com.
- CDISC (Clinical Data Interchange Standards Consortium). cdisc.org.

Open Data and Tools

- IMSA. "Official Race Results." results.imsa.com.
- OpenF1 API. "The Open Source API for Formula 1 Data." openf1.org.
- TracingInsights. "F1 Racing Analytics." tracinginsights.com.

Disclosure

Several technology vendors named in this book - including Modak, +tellic, Tamr, and Cloudera - were sponsors of the author's Big Data in Action racing program. They are discussed here because their platforms have been successfully deployed in the large-scale enterprise data solutions described in this book, not as paid endorsements. The author received no compensation for referencing any product, and the views expressed are his own.

www.ingramcontent.com/pod-product-compliance
Lightning Source LLC
LaVergne TN
LVHW010336220926
848484LV00004BB/912